THE YOGA OF POOL

Secrets to Becoming a Champion in Billiards and in Life

By Paul Rodney Turner
(BATman)

Inventor of the Billiard Aim Trainer™ (BAT)

The YOGA of POOL

© Copyright 2010 by Paul Rodney Turner.
All rights reserved.

First Printing 2010 (*How to Play Great Pool*)
USA

Date of Publication: June 14, 2012

ISBN: 978-0-9850451-0-4

Contents

Dedicated to my father, Rodney Turner,
the "Phantom" (1940–2001)

Introduction

If you're like me, you've probably read all the books on how to improve your game, including the classics from Phil Capelle. I don't propose that this book will cover every facet of the game of billiards; Capelle's books do a great job of that. However, what I will declare is that *The YOGA of POOL – Secrets to becoming a Champion in Billiards and in Life* will provide you **all the essential tools you need** to become a great player, while simultaneously helping to make you a better person.

The book provides the fundamental ingredients of what makes a great player. The chapters are concise and digestible and not filled with unnecessary fluff. The idea behind the book is to give you an easy-to-understand roadmap to success in the form of short essays describing key elements of the game.

I need to point out that the sections dealing with aiming are taken from my other book, *World's Best Aiming System for Billiards*. I felt it was necessary to include the same information for completeness of this book. If you already purchased my other book the *World's Best Aiming System for Billiards*, you may skip those sections. In any case, the knowledge contained within this book will certainly expand your understanding of the Three-Cut System and support your development in all other facets of the game.

One glaring omission from many books on billiards is a lack of information on the mental and spiritual side of the game, including proven techniques for visualization, mind management, and confidence building exercises. You'll find them in this book, and rightly so, because to ignore the mind and spirit is akin to ignoring the driver of the vehicle. Every world-class motor racing team knows that a good driver is *the* difference between success and failure.

As the subtitle suggests, this book is much more than the secrets for success in billiards; it is, in a way, a kind of "Covey-like" directive for the billiards enthusiast on what makes one successful in life.

You may just come away from reading this book feeling a renewed sense of self-worth and optimism. I hope so. I promise you this: if you apply the following ingredients of success to your game, and in your life, **you will experience monumental improvements** in every aspect.

My hope is that the book will serve to make you the very best player and person you can possibly be.

You deserve it!

Paul Rodney Turner (BATman)

Manage Your Mind

The most important ingredient and therefore the first ingredient to becoming a great pool player is *managing your mind*. All the best fundamentals in the world will never compensate for a wayward or mischievous mind. You can have perfect alignment and know exactly what to do, but if your mind tells you "I can't get this," chances are you'll miss.

Success in any discipline begins in the mind. All the world's greatest monuments, masterpieces, songs, Olympic moments, and books on the *New York Times* bestseller list started with the right mindset. The point is that you must learn to see your success in your mind first, before you can expect to execute it in physical reality.

According to Eastern mystic traditions, the mind is the master of the senses, and therefore controls the physical actions and reactions of the body. All of us have at one time heard an amazing story of some person who was told they would never walk again, only for them to defy the odds and start running marathons. Lance Armstrong is a case in point: Bedridden for months, wracked with pain from the cancer spreading throughout his body and brain, he never considered failure an option, and with a level of determination that would be impossible for most, he fully recovered and went on to win seven *Tour de France* titles. In every example, those people who were able to surmount great physical obstacles have done so with the help of their minds. In other words, they ran that marathon over and over again in their mind, and then one day they actually played out that vision.

The same truth applies in pool; we have to see ourselves pocketing balls effortlessly in our mind. We have to actually envision escaping hooks with the greatest skill and confidence. With full clarity of mind, we have to see ourselves raising that trophy, accepting the prize money, being congratulated for a great win – and we have to truly believe that it is all fully possible. If you want to be successful in pool, you must embrace positive thinking as if it is your only option.

The mind can be your worst enemy or your best friend. It is completely up to you because you (the soul), as the *driver* of your vehicle (the body), *always has a choice.* How so? The *Bhagavad Gita* explains:

> *The working senses are superior to dull matter; mind is higher than the senses; intelligence is still higher than the mind; and he [the soul] is even higher than the intelligence.[1]*

The basic function of the intelligence is to discriminate – a sort of "yes or no" function. Much like a complex computer is nothing but a series of on and off sequences or ones and zeros, the intelligence is giving a thumbs-up or a thumbs-down to literally millions of situations and processes inside and outside of our bodies daily, most of them without our conscious awareness.

Above the intelligence, however, is the presence of consciousness or spirit – the "I" factor – the sense-of-being we all have, regardless of our physical or mental status. This sense-of-being or inherent spirituality, is what makes us unique individuals, and is indeed the very essence of our existence. This consciousness or core identity is what determines all our actions. Essentially, if you can connect to your core identity, you *can* have full power over your mind.

Start to see your mind, therefore, as *the* most important tool for improving your game. Never again allow it dictate to you through negative thought patterns that only serve to consume your energy and sap your will. Rather, fully believe in the best possible outcome and tell your mind what *you* want it to do. Use your higher intelligence and free will to direct your mind to positive thoughts of success, confidence, and empowerment.

In fact, never underestimate the importance of managing your mind in every aspect of your life. How we relate to pool and the

---

[1] *Bhagavad Gita (Verse 3.42)*

way we respond to our success or failure in this game can easily be correlated to the way we conduct ourselves in our daily affairs.

When you understand the power of the mind to positively impact your physical experience, and know that *you* actually have the power to direct it, you align yourself with all the greatest thinkers, artists, and athletes in history. Every single one of them had or displayed great mind management.

How do we actually start to manage the mind?

The first thing is to start *paying attention*. Carefully note how your mind is reacting to things that happen to you when playing. Like a detached observer, start listening to what your mind's current chatter is. Make a concerted effort to separate yourself from what your mind is saying, by being the "observer". Carefully listen to the self-talk going on and then, if necessary, slowly start correcting it. The good news is that the mind can always be trained, no matter how old your physical body is! Don't be discouraged with your technique at this point; just start making a sincere effort. Good mind management will enable you to make better choices as well, and every good choice is a step in the direction of success. Success will breed more success, and soon you will be rolling along with an air of confidence you cannot even imagine right now.

The best way to correct negative thinking (which some call "stinking thinking") is to replace it with "success thinking". Earl Nightingale, considered the *Dean of personal development*, used to say, "*We become what we think about all day long.*" On the surface, this sounds like magic, but if we investigate this concept further, we'll find it has merit. Success thinking always precedes a successful outcome, while failure-thoughts prepare us for failure.

For success thinking to yield results, you need to develop a positive attitude toward every aspect of your life. Expect a successful outcome in whatever you do, but also take any necessary actions to ensure your success.

9

Effective success thinking that brings results is much more than just repeating a few positive words or convincing yourself that everything is going to be okay. The idea of success has to become your predominant mental outlook. It is not enough to think positively for a few moments, and then allow fears and lack of belief enter your mind. Some effort and discipline are necessary.

Here are a few tips to help you develop the power of success thinking:

- Always use affirmative and positive phrases when you communicate and only speak in the present tense. For example, from this day on begin all your positive and affirmative statements with: I am; I always; I can; I am able to; I will.

- If you have to speak about some negative event, speak about it *only* in past tense. For example, you could begin your statements with: I used to; in the past; I have in the past; it was; it has, etc. **Never** speak of past mistakes or misfortune in the present tense.

- Completely ignore negative thoughts. Outright reject them and immediately substitute them with constructive happy thoughts.

- Use only words that evoke feelings and mental images of strength, happiness, and success.

- Before starting with any plan or action, visualize clearly in your mind its successful outcome.

- Read inspiring literature like the success stories of great athletes.

- Minimize your exposure to negative news. Even better, stop reading or watching the news on television altogether as most of it is negative. Rather, practice scanning headlines to keep abreast of current events.

- Seek out and associate with positive thinking people.

- Maintain a success posture. Always walk with your head up and your back straight. Posture is important because if the body is not properly aligned the voice can't come out with the power, resonance and projection that it naturally has.

- When you shake hands, do so with confidence and look the person directly in the eye.

- Regular exercise can also help you develop a more positive attitude, as can deep meditative breathing.

You have to start training your mind to think like a winner by speaking like a winner. By simply changing the way you perceive yourself, you can expect and will allow good things to happen.

Just as sound can be the seed of creation or destruction, a single thought can be the seed of inspiration or discouragement. Each World War began with words, and every great achievement began with someone voicing their dream to a friend. Success has to be believed before it can be achieved.

When we think negatively we sow seeds of discouragement, which are initially expressed as negative talk. This negative talk sends our minds on a downward spiral and keeps us struggling. However, when we choose to be proactive, positive, and hopeful, and to exemplify this with confident speech patterns, we sow seeds of inspiration that in turn produce more confident body language and positive actions. These progressive actions germinate seeds of encouragement that fuel our belief, thus leading to a happier life and greater achievement.

The next time you miss a shot while playing pool, instead of losing your cool and claiming: "I am useless, I always miss," say to yourself: "I may have missed this time, but I am fully confident that I can make these shots." Then slowly replace these positive excuses with positive affirmations, like: "I always shoot straight; I am a great shot maker; I know how to run out; I am a winner; I was born to win; when I play pool, the balls always roll in my favor." Practice this on and off the table. You may like to incorporate other affirmations to help you in other areas of your life. Thoughts are things and so the pictures you form in your mind will eventually manifest in physical reality.

Therefore, start making your mind your best friend and not your worst enemy. The *Bhagavad Gita* explains:

> *A man must elevate himself by his own mind, not degrade himself. The mind is the friend of the conditioned soul, and his enemy as well. For him who has conquered the mind, the mind is the best of friends; but for one who has failed to do so, his very mind will be the greatest enemy.*[2]

A mind that has been nourished with positive affirmations will automatically react positively like a true friend and be the source of inspiration for a perfect solution.

The best way to neutralize the "darkness" of negative thinking and any hint of fear residing in your mind is to allow the sunshine of positivity to stream in! In other words, if you fill your mind with light, there will be no place for darkness to reside.

Mind/Body oneness

It is true that through the power of mind management we can affect physical reality; however, because we are ultimately a combination of both gross and subtle energy (*yin* and *yang*), it is also true that the mind will follow what the body tells it.

Buddhist monk Thich Nhat Hanh explains that by nurturing the oneness of body and mind, and by listening to our body, "we are able to restore our wholeness .... and as body and mind become one, we need only to calm our body in order to calm our mind."

Just like the body, we need to feed and exercise the mind. Success talk is an effective way to do that. However, for this method to be truly effective, you must first understand that *the mind is not you*, but rather just another tool at your disposal that can either help you or hurt you. It can be your friend or your enemy. It's your

---

[2] *Bhagavad Gita As It Is (Verse 6.5 and 6.6)*

choice. Just as a knife in the hands of a criminal can be dangerous, that same knife in the hands of a trained surgeon can save a life. The knife is neither good nor bad; it is how we use it that matters. The same goes for the mind. Make it your friend from now on; believe in yourself and start playing great pool!

The perfect yogi is of "steady mind" says the *Bhagavad Gita*:

> One who is not disturbed in spite of the threefold miseries[3], who is not elated when there is happiness, and who is free from attachment, fear and anger, is called a sage of steady mind.[4]

In the same way, a great pool player will be a master of his mind and will never become disturbed if behind in game or overly elated if he is in front. Free from attachment, fear and anger, his mind will be as calm as a great lake.

Later in the book, I will provide some confidence building exercises using techniques borrowed from Neural-Linguistic programming and other mind/body disciplines.

In the next chapter, we are going to focus more on the practical side of improving your game, beginning with learning the world's best aiming system.

---

[3] *Threefold miseries are the miseries pertaining to the body and mind, miseries caused by other living entities, and miseries resulting from natural disaster.*
[4] *Bhagavad Gita (verse 2.56)*

The Three-Cut System

The aiming system used by the world's most successful players in all cue sports is most commonly referred to as the "Three-Cut System". Simply put, it is the most scientific aiming system there is, and it's based on pure geometry. There are really only three cuts you need to learn to master pocketing balls. They are: ¼, ½ and ¾ cuts. All other cuts shots are slight variations of these three.

In geometry, the degrees of the angle these cuts correspond to are:

¼ = 49 ° (degrees)

½ = 30 ° (degrees)

¾ = 14 ° (degrees)

The basis of this aiming system is to imagine the object ball having four equal slices, beginning with a perfect slice down the middle representing two halves of a ball and then to the left and right of the ½ ball slice, thus creating the ¼ and ¾ ball slice (Figure 1).

Basically, this aiming method is to first identify the degree of the angle the object ball needs to take to enter the desired pocket, and then use one of these three "cuts" as our point of reference for aiming. However, as I will explain shortly, the edge of the ball is always our principle reference.

How this method works becomes clear once we apply the same "cut lines" to the cue ball and then superimposing our cue ball over the object ball, as if both were flat "paper balls"5. (Figure 2)

The edge is the only true reference point

It is extremely important to understand this one truth: on a perfectly spherical object like a billiard ball the only absolute

---

5 *For this exercise it might be useful to actually cut out two equal-sized paper circles to represent a cue ball and an object ball.*

reference is the edge. Absolute from the point of view of the observer, that is, which in our example, is from the point of view looking at the object ball directly behind your cue ball.

The half-ball cut shot

How is it possible that the only true reference point on a spherical object is its edge? Because every "point" on a ball is always relative to the position of the observer. In other words, as you move around the table, the edge of a ball changes relative to your observation of it. In truth, a ball does not really have an "edge" but rather a surface, but staying with our example of "paper balls" we will refer to the outer line of the intended object ball as having an "edge".

In billiards, because the object ball and cue ball are the same size, the "edge" of the object ball (from the viewpoint of your cue ball) represents a perfect "half-ball" cut shot, and therefore an excellent reference for determining all other cut shots. Knowing that a perfect "half-ball" cut is a collision of the cue ball and object ball at a 30° degree angle[6] can be a tremendous advantage over your opponent. Because once your eyes have been trained to recognize this 30° degree angle, you'll automatically know that your point of aim is the outside line or "edge" of that object ball. In other words, your cue tip and the center of your cue ball must be pointed directly at the left or right "edge" of the desired object ball to successfully send it on the correct path (30° degree angle) towards the pocket. It really is that simple.

One crude way to estimate a 30° angle when playing pool is to create a "V" or peace symbol with your first two fingers (Figure 4a). With practice, and by using training tools like the Billiard Aim Trainer (BAT™), estimating 30° angles becomes very easy.

To sum up: from the point of view of your cue ball the far left and right "edge" of the object ball represent perfect ½ ball cuts either

---

[6] *Basic geometry tells us that 30° is one-third of a perfect right angle (90°). Use this information as a reference when trying to recognize a half-ball cut shot when you next play.*

way (Figure 3). In other words, by aiming the center of your cue ball directly at either "edge" of the object ball you will send that object ball on a perfect 30° degree angle. Therefore, if you analyzed the angle correctly (which you will with practice), you'll pocket the ball every time! The same rules apply for all other cut shots in a game, whether they are ¼, ½ or ¾, or slight variations of them. (Figure 4 and Figure 5).

I suggest you begin with the ½ ball cut and progress from there. The best way to learn this system and to start recognizing the three angles correlating to the ¼, ½ and ¾ cut shots is by using the Billiard Aim Trainer. However, even without the BAT™, by simply employing the ½ ball cut shot into your game, you will build a solid foundation for all other cut shots.

An example of a ¾ ball cut shot is shown in (Figure 4) To make the object ball move on a 14° degree path, we simply need to adjust our aim to exactly (¼ of a ball) inside the edge of the object ball. The same rule applies for a ¼ ball cut shot, only this time we adjust our aim to a (¼ of a ball) outside the edge of the object ball (Figure 5) thus sending it on a 49° degree path. In both cases, the edge of the object ball is our reference and not some imaginary "ghost ball". This one point alone should convince you of the superiority of the Three-Cut system.

Cue Tip Reference

If you find it difficult to visualize this distance (¼ of a ball) you may use your cue tip as a reference (Figure 6). In our examples, the cue ball is 2¼ inches wide or 57mm, which is a standard size pool ball used in the United States, so the distance between these "cut lines" would therefore be 14.25mm.

From this illustration, we can see that a typical cue tip used in pool is 13mm wide, and therefore a good reference when estimating these 14.25mm (¼ and ¾ ball) "cut lines". It may be hard to visualize a distance of 14.25mm, but it is relatively easy for any pool player to visualize a fraction more than the width of their cue tip! And certainly a lot easier than an imagining a "ghost ball" on the table that has no reference point to start with. Worse still, the imaginary positioning of this "ghost ball" in relation to the object ball could be completely wrong, and if you are wrong, there is absolutely no way to correct this the next time you shoot. Quite simply, the entire "ghost ball" aiming system is based on imagining something (the cue ball) being positioned at a particular point on the table based on our assumption of what angle of trajectory is needed to send our object ball to the pocket. And if we're wrong we just have to guess again. There is nothing to measure our success or failure against.

On the contrary, once you learn the three angles of the Three-Cut system, there is never any question of being perpetually wrong because you will always have the edge of the object ball as your reference.

To train your eyes to recognize these three angles (49°, 30°, and 14° degrees) I have given a number of training drills in the back section of this book.

FIGURE 1

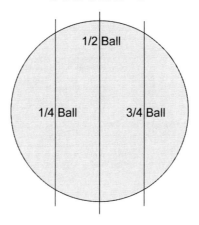

FIGURE 2

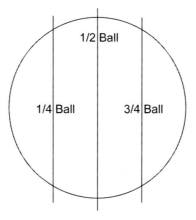

FIGURE 3

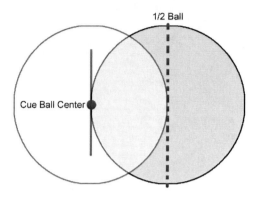

1/2 Ball

Cue Ball Center

1/2 BALL CUT

FIGURE 4

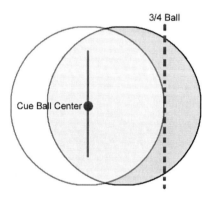

3/4 Ball

Cue Ball Center

3/4 BALL CUT

FIGURE 4a

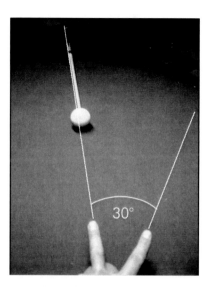

The above picture shows my hand over the orange object ball, with my middle finger pointing directly down the line of the cue ball and my arm and pointer finger directly in line with the pocket I wish the orange ball to go into. It is the classic "spot shot" explained in (See Figure 13 for more details).

FIGURE 5

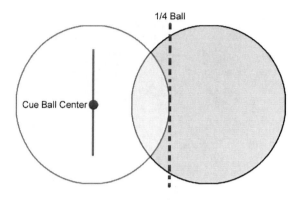

1/4 BALL CUT

FIGURE 6

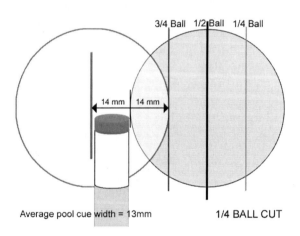

1/4 BALL CUT

Aim While Standing

All aiming should be done from the standing position. Once you are down to play, your only thought should be to execute the shot as precisely as possible in order to pocket the ball and get the best possible position on the next. All aiming adjustments should be over once you are down for the shot. If you find you're making adjustments and double guessing the shot while down, stand up immediately and start all over again. All good professional players do this. Therefore, it is essential that you learn the same discipline if you want to be a great shot maker.

A common mistake most amateurs make while playing pool is to get down too quickly to shoot, without first carefully surveying all aspects of the shot, namely:

(1) The degree of angle to pocket the object ball;

(2) The natural tangent path of the cue ball; and

(3) The positional zone in which you need to leave the cue ball after pocketing the current object ball.

Let's look at all three, one by one.

The Degree of the Angle

Why do people always want a top-floor view? Because only from the top floor do you get the best perspective of the entire area. In the same way, when we observe the layout of the pool table from the standing position, we are better able to see potential run-out patterns, and more importantly, we can better estimate the degree of the angle of the cut to pocket our next ball. In other words, from the standing position we can best estimate whether the angle of the path the object needs to take to enter the pocket will require a ¼, ½ or ¾ ball cut shot, or a slight variation of one of them.

The next time you are at the table, get behind the shot you are considering and then compare what you can see in the standing

23

position to what you can see when you are down on the shot. The fact is: if you have not already carefully noted the angle to the pocket from the standing position, your perception will be greatly hindered from the table level viewpoint. So this is the first rule when aiming.

The Three-Cut System explained in the previous chapter emphasizes the need to familiarize yourself with just three standard cut shots: namely ¼, ½, and ¾ ball cuts. Again, these three cuts correspond to the following angles: 49°, 30°, and 14° degrees, respectively. I understand, however, that for most amateur players this may still be confusing. After all, how do you accurately estimate these angles while playing pool? Well, practice makes perfect, but one way to see these angles while playing is to use the visual references depicted in Figure 7, 8, and 9) or to familiarize yourself by training with tools like the *Billiard Aim Trainer (BAT™)*.

By familiarizing yourself with these images, or by training with the BAT™ it will become very easy to recognize these standard cut angles while playing. Commit these images to memory and try to see them as you survey the table the next time you play.

FIG 7

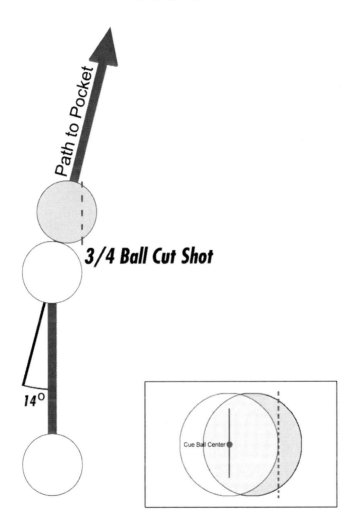

Path to Pocket

3/4 Ball Cut Shot

14°

Cue Ball Center

FIG 8

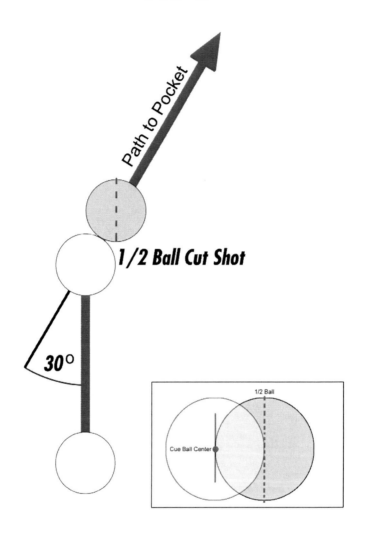

Path to Pocket

1/2 Ball Cut Shot

30°

1/2 Ball

Cue Ball Center

FIG 9

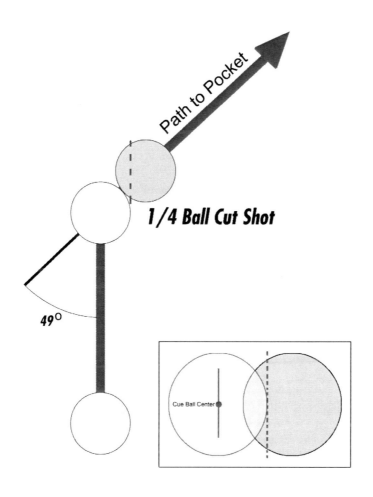

Path to Pocket

1/4 Ball Cut Shot

49°

Cue Ball Center

The Natural Tangent Path

The next bit of information we need to gather while in the standing position is the potential tangent path of the cue ball after contact with the object ball. The cue ball always starts out on the tangent line after contact with the object ball, but then the rolling speed and the amount of English (side spin) on the cue ball determines where it goes thereafter. The harder the cue ball is struck, the longer it will stay on the tangent line, regardless of the forward, backward, or side rotation. We can easily visualize the tangent path by placing our cue stick perpendicular to the impact point on the object ball to show the 90° angle. It is impossible to accurately estimate the tangent from the table level position, so we should take the time to look over the ball we are attempting to pocket to identify this 90° angle or tangent. Knowing the tangent will greatly help in deciding how to stroke the cue ball to avoid potential scratches[7] or unwanted collisions with other balls on the table.

The next time you play, make it a habit before every shot to walk around the table and see the shot from different angles, so that what could potentially happen after the shot has been played out in your mind first. Over time, it will not always be necessary to walk around the table to visualize the tangent path, because your knowledge of cue ball pathways around the table will become second nature.

How to See the Tangent Line

1. Stand directly behind the object ball in line with pocket you wish to put it in.
2. You can visualize the approximate tangent path of the cue ball by making an "L" sign with your thumb and index finger to represent a crude 90° degree angle.
3. If you are shooting from the right side, use your right hand. If your cue ball is to the left of the object ball, use your left hand in this exercise.

---

[7] A "scratch" in US billiards terminology is the same as an "Inn-off" in English billiards, or when the cue ball goes into a pocket.

4. Your index finger will represent the path of the object ball to the pocket, and your thumb will now show the potential tangent path of the cue ball.

Note: The tangent path of the cue ball is the theoretical path of a cue ball that has no spin applied to it. In other words, it is sliding at the time it contacts the object ball.

The **actual** tangent path of the cue ball will vary depending on the amount of forward or backward spin remaining on the cue ball. Forward spin = decreased angle (< less than 90° degrees). Back spin = increased angle (great than 90° degrees).

Length of the Tangent

To estimate the length of the tangent path of the cue ball, or the distance it will travel after contact with the object ball, we simply need to use the following formula: [Power of the shot] – [percentage of the object ball being hit] = distance the ball will travel. Or Power – Percentage = Distance. Or simply Pw-Pc=D.

For example, say you hit the cue ball with enough power for it to go the length of the table, but you made a ½ ball cut shot, the answer would be:

[Length-of-Table Power] – [50%] = half the table length.

The power of the shot (100%) has been split between the object ball and the cue ball. This would mean that the object ball would also travel half the length of the table.

If on the other hand, you feathered a shot, as in the case of a 1/8 of a ball cut shot, and assuming you hit the ball with the same power (length of table) as before, the formula would read:

[Length of table] – [1/8 or 12.5% of the ball] = 7/8 or 87.5% of the length of the table. The object ball would only travel 12.5% of that length. The power you employed has been split between the two balls.

Another way to understand this is to remember that whatever power you put on the shot will be taken away by the object ball on contact. If you hit a full ball, the object ball will take 100% of that power, but if you hit only half of the object, it will only take 50% of that power. The remaining power will stay on the cue ball and make it travel a certain distance. Getting to accurately estimate this distance takes practice.

Of course, this formula does not take into consideration any *English*[8] that you might intentionally or unintentionally apply to the cue ball. It is a basic formula to be used to estimate the distance the cue ball travels.

The Exact Positional Area

Lack of position play is the greatest mistake amateur players make. Without considering the position of the cue ball after the shot, it is near impossible to ever run a rack.[9] Sooner or later, if you are negligent in this part of your game, your run outs will consistently stop as you get deeper and deeper into trouble and find yourself facing some heroic, low percentage shot to keep the run going. What most amateur players forget to realize is that as their object balls disappear, so do their options. This is particularly evident in a game of eight ball, and so it is not uncommon to see a less advanced player get beaten at the "finish line" because the other player's balls were blocking opportunities to win. One of the greatest tricks in eight ball is to use your balls like "soldiers" and block your opponent's access to pockets. A game of eight ball is never truly over until the black ball goes down. So never be discouraged if you find yourself apparently "behind".

Have you ever noticed how professional players seem to make the game look easy, as they magically find themselves with easy shots all the time? It is not by chance. They have carefully considered their position play and have executed accordingly. Most top players will actually run the entire rack in their mind, immediately

---

[8] *Sidespin or "English" is created on the cue ball when it is struck off-center, which in most circumstances, can also affect the direction of the object ball.*
[9] *Running a rack means pocketing all balls on the table necessary to win a game in one visit to the table.*

following the break, before they get down to play their first shot! That is position play at its best.

So during your analysis of the table layout from the standing position, take a moment to map out your pathway for a potential run out and keep in mind positional zones[10], and not just points on the table. Granted, if your stroke play is so advanced that you can literally position your cue ball on command, like Efren Reyes, then go for it. But it is better to play the higher odds, and aim for positional zones rather than points on the table (Figure 24).

Position play is much easier to estimate and control once you have carefully surveyed the table from the "top floor". Careful position play always takes into account the natural tangent path of the cue ball and the subsequent natural path the cue ball takes as it bounces off the cushions. You have to see this path in your mind before you get down to play your shot. Play this shot perfectly in your mind first. Actually see the ball being pocketed and then see the cue ball traversing a natural path and stopping in an area of the table that is perfect for your next shot.

Incorporate these three tips into your play and reap the benefits. But remember, they all depend on taking the time to first analyze the shot while standing. So, aim while standing.

---

[10] *Positional zones are optimal areas on the table where you would like your cue ball to land within after completing your shot. Position zones typically appear as a triangular shape, so it is best to make your cue ball enter them from the narrow side.*

Back Foot First
(Proper body alignment)

Like any other ball sport, billiards requires that players use their feet correctly. Can you imagine Roger Federer, a right-handed tennis player, going for a backhand winner with his left foot in front of his right? It just wouldn't happen. The same principle applies in boxing; your lead hand always follows your lead foot. Correct foot placement is crucial to proper execution in games and martial sports. Indeed, Muhammad Ali, considered the greatest boxer of all time, was famous for his great footwork, especially the "Ali shuffle". The same principle of correct foot placement applies to golf, basketball, bowling, and of course billiards.

So what *is* the correct placement of the feet when playing billiards? Well, if you're anything like myself, you've read a whole bunch of books depicting the correct placement, but more than likely you've also noticed that there are differing opinions. Still, one thing remains certain: all teachers agree that your stance needs to be solid and balanced.

That said, I want to tell you a secret about how using your back foot for aiming can improve your overall accuracy tenfold! Let me explain ...

Just like our tennis player example, no matter how good you are at hitting the ball, or how good your eye-hand coordination is, if you are not correctly aligned with the shot, the ball will not go where you intend. In other words, it is your *body alignment,* specifically the placement of your back foot, that determines the path of the cue ball, far more than your stroke does. Yes, I said your **back foot!** This is a fundamental difference between billiards and all other sports in which foot placement is important.

In billiards, it is simply not enough to have the fundamentals of a good stance and then not pay attention to how your feet are aligned in relation to the shot. And the most important foot in this regard is your back foot. For a right-handed player, this is your right foot.

Once you have surveyed the table and calculated the angle of the shot, as explained in *Aim While Standing*, you absolutely must get the inside of your back foot in line with the path you wish to send the cue ball on. That means, in your mind, extend a line from the object ball through the cue ball and then towards your back foot, and place the inside of your back foot on that line. Then, and then only, drop down naturally into your stance.

Once the inside of your back foot is in line with the shot, step the other foot out and ahead of the back foot to a position that is both comfortable and stable. However, both feet should typically be shoulder width apart for balance. Depending on your body type, this position can vary dramatically.

You should feel completely rooted, like a tree, with your weight coming slightly forward. As you do this, you will naturally shift the majority of your weight to the front leg, which will then automatically move your hip away from your cue arm.

If you have done this correctly, you will find you are lined up perfectly to play the shot.

Modern snooker players tend to face the shot (Figure10a) so that both of their feet point in the same direction as the line of the shot, whereas most pool players tend to turn the back foot slightly out and place only the lead foot parallel to the cue stick (Figure 10b).

Both of these stances[11] work very well. You will notice that, either way, the *inside* of the back foot stays in line with the shot. The only difference is that one stance may be more comfortable for you, which is also very important. Allison Fisher's personal stance has her left foot slightly ahead of the right, with the right toe halfway up the left foot.

The position of the front foot is nowhere near as important as the back foot, which *absolutely* needs to be properly aligned. It is the key to correct aiming.

---

[11] *The feet alignment shown is for a right-handed player.*

Why? Because as soon as your back foot is aligned correctly with the desired path of the cue ball, your entire body will be as well. Once your body is correctly aligned, the mechanics of the shot delivery take over, and for any decent player it is relatively easy to play the shot, even with eyes closed.

As I mentioned earlier, in a traditional pool stance, a player will turn the back foot out and have the lead foot much further in front and angled. This is also typical of the old-fashioned snooker stance of the legendary Joe Davis. I also adhere to this style.

In both stances, your front knee should be slightly bent, and depending on your height, you may choose to bend the back leg slightly as well. There are no hard and fast rules on this because body types are so varied, and yet the pool table is generally a standard height from the floor. So *you* can decide on this, just as long as the stance is solid.

FIG 10

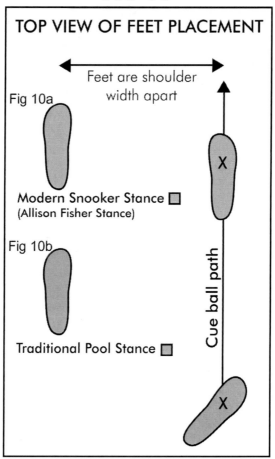

TOP VIEW OF FEET PLACEMENT

Feet are shoulder width apart

Fig 10a

Modern Snooker Stance ▫
(Allison Fisher Stance)

Fig 10b

Traditional Pool Stance ▫

Cue ball path

However, be careful not to lean back, because this will inevitably make you jump up on the shot. What you want from your stance is to be able to send the cue forward effortlessly while remaining rock steady. Placing your weight slightly on the leading leg will make this easier.

In a metaphysical sense, focusing on the placement of the back foot is akin to making sure you are on solid ground before advancing forward. "Charity begins at home," and so in billiards, you always want to make sure that you base your offense on solid ground.

Too often in life we jump to conclusions or follow the whims of the mind, without first thinking about our current circumstance or the consequences of our actions. It is better to take a moment to first affirm your position, by thinking carefully about your circumstances, before making haste. In billiards, as in life, thoughtfulness is well worth the investment.

In saying this, I do not want you to misinterpret my words as those of a naysayer—a pessimist. On the contrary, an optimistic outlook on life does not suggest irresponsibility or erratic behavior. Success comes when we have our goal fixed in our mind and we walk towards it day after day with a gait that is filled with confidence— every step being firm and resolute. Remember this: **a firmly placed back foot *always* precedes a successful step forward**.

The Yoga of Pool
(Body/mind connection & flexibility)

With all that talk about body positioning in the last chapter, it's time to limber up a bit.

The word "yoga" in its original sense has little to do with exercise, but in fact comes from the Sanskrit verb *yuj*, to yoke or unite.

Of course, we understand that the original intent has spiritual connotations and refers specifically to uniting with a higher source. But just for fun, let's use this same principle of yoga to help us improve our game by uniting our body and mind as one.

Yoga is balance—balance between the inner and outer life so as to obtain an awareness of your higher individuality. People who are always busy working, without thinking about themselves will feel incomplete, because they have severed a vital connection with the world by an overemphasis on one aspect of their being—either their mind or body.

As I mentioned in chapter one, you have to make your mind your best friend so that it works for you and not against you. You do this by first understanding that you always have a choice. According to the esoteric teachings of the East, essentially eight forms of energy constitute the material world: *Earth, water, fire, air, ether, mind, intelligence, and false ego.* Quantum physics concurs that when we break things down to their tiniest parts we are left with nothing but pure energy, both gross and subtle. So where do *we* fit into that picture? According to the *Bhagavad-gita*, above these eight gross and subtle energies is the soul or consciousness that is immutable and everlasting.

I am not going to get into a religious lecture here, but please stay with me. The absolute power of the soul is a common birthright of every living being. Despite our obvious physical difference, on the spiritual plane we are all equal in quality and therefore possess the same potential. Just like the sun illuminates and sustains this world, similarly, the spirit within animates the body. In both our physical and spiritual personas we are like the sun. Our physical bodies are made of the same material "stuff" as the stars, and within, we shine brightly via our consciousness.

The *Bhagavad-gita* explains:

> ... *as the sun alone illuminates all this universe, so does the living entity, one within the body, illuminate the entire body by consciousness.*[12]

> *One who knowingly sees this difference between the body and the owner of the body and can understand the process of liberation from this bondage, also attains to the supreme goal.*[13]

Understanding this difference is really not so difficult. We can practically experience the difference between the body, mind, intelligence, and consciousness, because even when the body is inactive, the mind will continue to act—as it does during dreaming. Since the power of discrimination that defines intelligence always has the ability to overrule any futile suggestions your mind comes up with, we must agree with the *Bhagavad-gita* that the intelligence is a finer form of energy. Above the intelligence, however, is the ultimate authority, the real *you*, the spirit or consciousness.

I can hear you asking: So how can understanding all this make me a great pool player? The key is to start using your intelligence to unite your mind with the actions of your body so that they act in perfect harmony. As the first chapter suggested, we must make our mind our friend, and if that means "beating" it into submission, so be it.

We achieve this in two ways: *Training & Affirmation*.

---

12 *Bhagavad-gita 13.34*
13 *Bhagavad-gita 13.35*

Disciplined Training

Through disciplined training and repetition of good results, much the same as you would discipline a young mischievous child, we can train our minds.

There is no doubt that practice makes perfect. The game of billiards, like any skill requiring great precision, requires serious practice and concentration. It is simply not good enough to knock some balls around every so often and consider that training. You have to work on drills, and when something works, you have to try to repeat it and firmly establish that skill in your mind and muscle memory.

Since the mind can be frivolous, it is best to establish a set time for such training, and some sort of routine. In the same way that you would discipline a naughty child, you have to take regulated disciplinary action with the mind. Set up a time, a place, and a routine that works best for you, and do it. Outside of that set time, have as much frivolity as you want, but during this time, you have to be serious. No excuses. It is this sort of discipline that defines a champion.

Affirmations

Monitoring your progress and writing down your realization is a wonderful way to train the mind and sharpen the intelligence. In the same way that you would monitor your achievements at the gym, note down how you are progressing in your training drills. You see, if you write something down you are going to be 10 times more effective in remembering and retaining that knowledge. And that is exactly what you want, because you have to *learn* from your mistakes and *remember what worked*. Mistakes can either haunt you forever or become moments of growth. The choice is always yours.

Writing down your realizations simply means capturing on paper those "eureka" moments when something makes sense for the first time: for example, the time you realized and experienced first-hand that playing your cue ball with one tip of inside *English* deflected the cue ball. Whatever little instance of illumination you experience, affirm it by writing it down, even if it is just a few words. Carry a pocket book to the poolroom and write it down.

Flexibility

Finally, this ingredient would not be complete if we did not address the importance of flexibility, which is of course another comparison with traditional yoga practice.

Although it is possible to play well without being able to turn your body into a pretzel, it is well documented in sports literature that having a flexible and toned body is a great advantage in any sport. In pool, flexibility is far more important than most players care to admit.

The fact is, the posture needed to play pool is not at all natural to the human body. There is nothing else in this world that requires you to assume such a bodily position as you do when playing pool. The same could be said of golf. So what does the world's number one golf player say about flexibility?

Although I have a lot of natural flexibility, I still work hard to maintain it. As we get older, our muscles tend to lose some of their elasticity... Every golfer should be concerned with maintaining suppleness in the shoulders, neck, back, chest, thighs and hips—all valuable power sources. [14]

– *Tiger Woods*

In a later chapter, I provide some flexibility and posture exercises that will both serve to make you more supple and, interestingly enough, also help to build your self-confidence.

---

[14] *Golf Digest, Feb, 2004 by Tiger Woods, Pete McDaniel*

The Rhythm of Success

We wonder at nature because of the rhythm and beauty of its movements. Every part of the wondrously complex and interdependent ecosystem plays like a symphony with every other part. There is a natural flow of energy, and harmony is what keeps it strong and enduring. When we upset that balance, however, problems occur, and we get results that we don't want. The horrors of global warming are a case in point, as mankind continues to upset the balance of Mother Earth and the natural flow of her loving energy.

In the same way, when we play pool, or any sport for that matter, we need to tune into our body's natural flow of energy and learn to develop a rhythm that best matches it. You and I are also nature. Every part of our body is composed of the same energy and substance as that which surrounds us. Learning to listen to our body and move in ways that create balance and rhythm will make us happier and more effective in whatever we do. This principle can be applied to every aspect of our lives, from diet to exercise to work and relaxation. All things must be balanced.

So how do we determine our natural rhythm when playing pool? We start by carefully observing what works. It is important that we don't just artificially copy someone else, but develop our own style, based on certain fundamental and proven principles that make up the rhythm of champions.

In nature, each tree finds its own way to the sun; each river finds its own way to the lake; and each species finds its own unique way to survive. In the same way, we have to recognize and honor our own individuality, all the while observing and learning from the success of others. A popular business strategy is to "copy success"; however, if we were to apply this principle to pool without respect for our own uniqueness, we would get lost in a blur of false identity. So learn from others, but be true to yourself.

The shot routine is the most fundamental part of a champion's arsenal. Every good player has one, and although there may be elements of similarity, each is uniquely theirs.

So what are the fundamental principles of a good shot routine?

Align

You decide on the path of your cue ball while in the standing position. Typically, you would do this from a point of view a little outside of the shot area, so that you get the best possible perspective on the shot.

Walk into the shot

Once you've analyzed the cut angle, decided on the aim, and identified the position you would like to cue ball to land, then, and then only, gently walk into the shot, all the while focused on exactly where you want to shoot the cue ball. It is at this time that you also align the inside of your back foot with the line of the shot. Doing so will allow you to place your cue, and then your body, on the correct line.

Tip to the cue ball

Once you're down for the shot, your first move is to place your cue tip at the cue ball. Then look down to do a final check that your alignment is correct. If it is not, get up, step back, and start over.

Warm up with rhythm

Here is where you see a lot of variation among players. I highly recommend you develop a rhythm to this part of the routine that suits your style, and then stick to it. Some players have a set number of back and forth strokes they always use, while others will match their eye movements by looking at the object ball on the backswing and the cue ball on the forward swing. With practice, this part of the routine will become automatic, and you can thus focus your entire attention on the delivery of the cue ball and its subsequent position once the shot is played.

Slow backswing

Often overlooked, a slow final backswing is critical for a smooth and consistent stroke. The practice is very common among snooker players, but still not so common in pool. A slow backswing will allow you to take full control of the execution and not fall prey to erratic strokes due to nerves. If you can only manage to incorporate one thing into your routine, do this one thing. It will do wonders for your accuracy and ball control. As you begin your final backswing, your eyes should slowly make the transition from the cue ball to the target.

Pause before the final delivery

Here, too, you will see a major difference in the stroke technique of snooker players and traditional pool players. All modern professional snooker players will pause at this stage. Ex-snooker players, like Allison Fisher, will pause as long as three seconds. I recommend that you pause for at least one second. It seems simple enough, but pausing at the critical moment before delivery is one of the hardest things to master in billiards. If you put in the time to incorporate a pause in your swing, your improvement will be significant. A full explanation of the pause will be described in the next chapter.

Fig 11

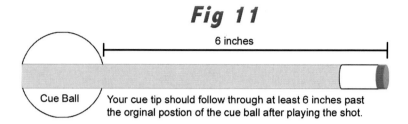

6 inches

Cue Ball / Your cue tip should follow through at least 6 inches past the orginal postion of the cue ball after playing the shot.

Follow through

Smoothly accelerate your cue through the cue ball, keeping your eyes fixed on the target, namely, the object ball. This ensures two things will happen: (a) there will be minimal or preferably no body movement; and (b) your cue tip will finish beyond the original position of the cue ball. The legendary Joe Davis had one of the sweetest strokes in snooker and his follow-through would often extend some 20 inches beyond the original position of the cue ball! The next time you play, take the time to measure how far your tip finished past the original position of the cue ball. At the very least, your follow through should be six inches as illustrated (Figure 11). Have a friend measure it for you, and if necessary continue to increase it until your pocketing improves.

Finish, wait, observe

Give yourself the best chance for accuracy by briefly holding your position after impact. Staying down on the shot for those few seconds until the cue ball comes to rest on the table allows you to: (a) greatly reduce your margin of error; and (b) analyze the shot to see whether it was perfect or if there was a flaw in execution, beginning with your stance.

Next we'll talk more about the importance of the pause in our stroke and how it literally is the "missing link" from most people's game.

The Pause

(Learning to transition)

That brief moment when the whole world seems to stand still – that temporary inaction while we focus on the future and prepare to commit our next move – is called a pause.

Why do we need this when playing pool?

Simply because, when we pause, we allow our energy and thoughts to collect and then to gracefully unwind into fruition. When we pause we create a moment of freedom in the mind, so that what comes next is pure poetry, and as natural as possible.

After every pause comes something anticipated and hoped for. We see this happen during a championship match when all of a sudden there is a tipping point—a change in the landscape when we all instinctively sense that something special is about to happen. It is the pivotal moment in a game when the crowd holds its breath and becomes silent, waiting. The atmosphere thickens with expectation as the next chapter of the event unfolds. What will happen? No one knows, but you can be sure that it was a *pause* that introduced that special moment.

Like the calm before the storm, the pause introduces the next event in our quest for victory. So embrace it, and use it to your advantage.

According to the dictionary, a pause is a point in time where there is inaction. I prefer to say that a pause represents a smooth transition between two points in time. For when we pause in our stroke, there is never a point of inaction but rather a slowing down of time as we move through our stroke.

I like to imagine a natural loop as the arm slows down until it appears to have stopped, but actually continues to loop gradually back in the tiniest of increments. There is no actual stop in the action but rather a continual, albeit very, very slow, smooth transition from backswing to forward stroke.

When we make a conscious effort to slow this part of our game down so that there is a pause on the final backswing, we allow the muscles to relax so that they can spring gracefully into action with the most natural and purest motion possible.

The art of pure motion is the science of transition from one position to the next, just as we see in the ballet dancer, the Jujitsu practitioner, or the professional racecar driver; all are working at every moment to achieve smooth transitions from one situation to the next.

The untrained eye may see erratic disconnections, but the expert will see the beauty and logic of each move. The same can be said of a smooth and graceful pool player, like Allison Fisher. Her technique is flawless and as smooth and flowing as a dancer. Moving from one shot to the next, she demonstrates cool, calm knowingness as she flows in and out of the table between each shot, pausing for exactly the same amount of time on every visit to the table. It is poetry in motion, and one cannot do better than to model this example of technique, attitude, and mindset.

In pool, the action of hitting a cue ball couldn't be simpler, and yet we tend to complicate things and allow our emotions and nerves to get in the way. If they do, you need to slow down, learn to relax and flow more. As I explained in the *Rhythm of Success*, you want to develop a rhythm around the table as you play. Good rhythm requires good transitions, and good transitions require a pause. It may be subtle, it may be brief, but it is *absolutely* essential.

Slow down, breath, flow, and pause before every major transition in your routine, of which the transition between the back swing and the final stroke is paramount.

Allison Fisher's pause before her final stroke certainly hasn't hurt her game!

A good way to gradually introduce a pause into your stroke is to practice pausing throughout your day. Before you eat, drink, or begin any completely new activity, you should briefly pause to reflect on the moment. Stop all mental chatter and just pause and exclusively focus on what you are about to do before you take action. By doing this you will train your mind to be more contemplative and less erratic. When you play billiards, this same habit should easily transfer over and you will find yourself feeling a greater sense of control at the table. In effect, the pause will help to remind yourself that you are in control; you are the driver of this vehicle we call the human body. By pausing, you are literally "resetting" your mental "operating system" and starting afresh.

Now that we have covered the fundamentals of a good technique, it's time to address attitude and how it is a critical component of a great player's arsenal.

Self-Respect and Will to Win

In a game of poker it is not uncommon for players to wear sunglasses to hide their eyes. Why? Because in poker, the eyes can speak volumes about a player's confidence. This is also true in boxing. Have you ever watched a stare-down at a boxing match? The two combatants stare at each other with such ferocity that it seems like the fight has already begun. Indeed it has! A slight turning down of the eyes or glance away is a sure sign of fear or doubt. Seemingly, one guy has already won the bout before even throwing a punch.

The next time you're watching *Rocky III*, take note of the stare-down between Rocky and Mr. T. In their first encounter, Rocky looks down, clearly showing weakness. Soon after, Mr. T. blasts him out of the ring in three brutal rounds. He takes a beating like never before, which all began at the stare-down. Rocky lost before the first punch was thrown.

In their next match, however, Rocky has regained his "eye of the tiger" and at the prefight stare-down he beams with unbridled confidence, looking Mr. T squarely in the eyes with an intensity saturated with confidence. This time it is Mr. T who looks down, revealing his own self-doubt. Rocky goes on to win and regain the championship.

Mike Tyson revealed that he was actually scared to fight people most of the time, but he never allowed the other fighter to know it. "I would always try to intimidate them and beat them before the fight," he said. "During the stare- down, if that fighter looked away for even a moment I knew I had him."

What we can learn from this is that a battle can be won or lost before the bell even sounds. The same rule applies in the relatively passive world of billiards. Unconsciously, two opponents size each other up, watching how the other reacts to certain situations in a game. It is these reactions, your facial expression, body language, and the things you say that reveal everything to your opponent and can possibly give them the upper hand. So what can you do about this? Think Vegas baby ... and put on your poker face!

When you "air dirty laundry" you reveal way too much information about your state of mind and skill level, and this can become a huge advantage for your opponent. For example, if you get visibly upset when you get hooked[15], a smart opponent will hook you again and again until you break. Any discriminating player will look for the weakness in an opponent's game; it is common knowledge in martial arts that you can win by focusing on your opponent's weak point.

Archimedes once said:

> Give me a place to stand and with a lever I will move the whole world.

The "place to stand" in this context is the weak point of your opponent's game. The "lever" is the strategy you adopt to exploit that weakness.

So if you want to keep your opponent guessing and respectful of you, never give away free information. Keep your inner game to yourself, and never reveal your game plan or your discomfort at any time during a game. You see, nothing is more frustrating than not knowing what your opponent is thinking, or finding them completely unflustered when you are dominating. Players who keep cool and focused and reveal no weaknesses or apparent concern, despite being behind on the scoreboard, send a clear message to their opponents that they are totally in control of the situation and remain a very real threat.

Keeping your opponents guessing achieves at least one thing: you have them focused on *you* instead of their own game, which can lead them eventually to make a mistake. A game that seems lost can

---

[15] *Being "hooked" is when your cue ball is obstructed by your opponent's balls. It is the same as being "snookered" in English billiard terminology.*

quickly turn, and suddenly you are making a comeback as your opponent's confidence erodes and doubts creep in. Your poker-face style will further fuel the situation as your opponent loses focus and their lead dwindles.

So never underestimate the power and influence of your body language, words, and facial expressions. When the going gets tough, refocus and remind yourself that you are a winner. Always conduct yourself like a winner. Soon you will be winning more often, and no one will be the wiser.

Will to Win

We all know by practical experience that we possess a "second-wind." Meaning, if we resolutely stick to a certain task, eventually any feelings of physical distress will subside, and we will capture a "second-wind." It appears that this "second-wind" comes about when we tap into our reserve store of vital energy or latent physical power. Every athlete is aware of this peculiar physiological phenomenon, when on the brink of exhaustion, a rush of new life surges through their veins.

A careful examination of this phenomenon reveals a curious parallel between the workings of Nature on the mental plane and the physical. Just as there is a physical "second-wind," there appears to be a mental reserve force from which we can harness to get a fresh start. For example, we may feel jaded while performing some tedious mental task, but as soon as we begin to feel that we are fully immersed in the activity, lo and behold, the "sails of our mind" catch a "second-wind" and we are once more able to perform our endeavor with a freshness, vigor and enthusiasm far surpassing the original effort.

Sometimes, however, we are unaware of these reserve mental energies that lay dormant within, and we go through life at a customary gait, believing that we are doing our best and getting all we can out of life. But the truth is, we are living only in the infancy of our mental capabilities, for behind that workman-like mentality rests stores of incredible mental power just awaiting the command of our *Will*. We are far greater beings than we care to realize. We may have a small physical frame, but within we are giants. Anthony Robbins talks of "awakening the giant within", as an expression of our inner potential. Author of *The Secrets of Success*, William Walter Atkinson explains:

> We are like young elephants that allow themselves to be mastered by weak men, and put through their paces, little dreaming of the mighty strength and power concealed within their organisms. We wonder at the achievements of the great men in all walks of life, and we are apt to excuse ourselves by the sad remark that these people seem to "have it in them," while we have not. Nonsense, we all have it in us to do things a hundred times greater than we are doing.

The source of this problem, Atkinson says is "desire, interest, and incentive to arouse into activity those wonderful storehouses of dynamic power within ..."

Usually we only tap into that power at times of great stress or urgency. Suddenly, seemingly out of nowhere, something within you disregards all apparent barriers and carries you into a state of focused action whereby you are able to accomplish tasks deemed impossible before.

Earnestness and enthusiasm are two great factors in harnessing these latent forces and dormant powers of the mind. But you need not artificially work yourself into a fit of fervor before these energies arise. "Through careful training of the *Will*, you can learn to manage the "mental throttle," and use it whenever necessary," he says.

The term "*Will*," means a firm steadfastness of mind or fixity of purpose. But it also means the "essential acting force of the mind"—capable of dominating and ruling all other mental faculties, as well as affecting anyone that comes within its field of influence.

Remember that true heroism is endurance for one moment more. That one moment more tells the difference between the "quitter" and the player who has done his best. Just like no one is determined dead until their heart has ceased beating, in the same way, no one has truly failed so long as there remains fight in him. That "one moment more" is often the moment in which the tide turns—the moment when the other player relaxes his mental grasp and drops his cue, as if already beaten.

Of all the mental powers, that of the *Will* is the closest to the sense of "I" or ego of the person. It is quite literally the "Sword of Power" clasped in the hand of the ego. It is *the* force with which you should rule your mental and physical kingdom. And when you do, your true Individuality will shine upon the outside world. Therefore cultivate your Will to win through disciplined training of the mind and a healthy sense of self worth.

Using the Will Proactively

It is wrong to apply your Will to anyone else. It is wrong to force others to do things for you. You don't need to apply your Will for things to come to you. It would be like trying to compel God to give you things. Unfortunately we see this happening during Christmas when people present a "shopping list" to God. Don't "pimp" your Will in this way. Rather, use your willpower on yourself *only*, by holding your actions to the desired course. Do not project your Will out, but rather use your mind to form a mental image of what *you want* and hold it with faith and purpose. As your clear intention radiates out into the universe, it will set off a chain of reactions and circumstances that will bring your desire to you. On the contrary, every moment you spend in disbelief of your desire, sets a current of energy "road blocks" to your inner desires manifesting. It is by your Will that you determine what *you* want. Success in any endeavor, including billiards, is not possible if your thoughts are filled with failure or frivolously moving from one goal to the next. Do not talk about failure. Do not think of past mistakes. Do not spend your time meditating or focusing on things that are diametrically opposite of success. Do not read, listen to, watch, or contemplate anything that creates mental images of failure. By your Will, keep your mind fixed on positivity and use it to feed your clearly defined goal.

"The poor do not need charity, they need inspiration," says Atkinson. Charity only helps these people temporarily. If you wish to help the poor, inspire them by your example. By the "tide" of your Will and passion, raise them to a higher level. Similarly, use your willpower to keep your mind off failure and fixed with faith and purpose on what *you* truly *want*.

Continuing with this theme, we will now look at how to conduct yourself when you're *not* at the table.

Staying Centered
(Don't play your opponent's game)

The next time you play a match, take careful note of your thoughts while you wait your turn to shoot. Like most people, I'll bet you are focusing either on your missed opportunity or how your opponent is surveying the table and executing their shot. The internal monologue will go something like this:

"I can't believe I just missed that shot ... That could cost me the match ... Is he going to play safe or go for it? If he goes for it and misses, what sort of opportunity is he going to leave me? What's taking him so long to shoot? Why did he play it that way? It's not fair, he's getting all the rolls ..."

This monologue is self-defeating, because in over-analyzing your missed shot or attempting to read the thoughts or actions of your opponent, you lose focus on your own game. The fact is: the view from your chair will never be as good as your opponent's, who can circle the table and see the entire layout. Moreover, the other player's selections are never as important as your own, since you have absolutely *no* control over them! So why waste your energy critiquing? Your mental gymnastics have absolutely no bearing on your opponent's actions, but only serve to hinder your performance and preparation for your next visit to the table. So why bother?

It is far better to use the time to center your thoughts on *your* game and completely rid yourself of any negative thoughts that may linger from having just lost control of the table. It *is* important to take a brief moment to analyze why you missed or executed a shot poorly, but don't hold onto these thoughts. Let them go. There are some worthwhile trains of thought while you wait to get back to the table, however, and circumstances will dictate which option is most suitable.

First of all, keep your focus and attention on your *own* match, and don't allow your thoughts to stray to outside factors you cannot control.

Next, visualize the table and shot selection as if you were still shooting. Never get caught up in critiquing or wishful thinking while your opponent is playing, but rather analyze the shot as if *you* had to make it. What would you do? If your opponent gets out of line or somehow lucky, stay focused and think about how you would play the next shot. In other words, in your mind, get back to the table as soon as possible. But do so with an attitude of utter confidence and calm, and on your own terms.

Take the opportunity to relax your mind, regulate your breathing, and fully prepare yourself for your next turn at the table. Recharge your body and revive your confidence with positive self-talk. If you wish to visualize scenarios in your head, recall those times when you played like a champion and had full confidence around the table. Pump yourself up and get ready for your turn.

One technique you may wish to utilize is known as "anchoring". It goes like this: remember a game winning shot you made in the past. Once you have totally immersed yourself in that memory and can feel a sense of satisfaction and confidence building inside you, do some simple action with your hand that you can associate with or "anchor" to that experience. In other words, make a connection between something simple you can do at any moment, like firmly pressing your index finger to your thumb. Do this while reliving the positive experience in your mind. Continue to do this over and over again until you have fully connected, or "anchored", these two experiences together. Then, when you find yourself struggling with confidence, privately make this secret gesture. If you have done this correctly, you will soon start reliving that memorable moment and experiencing the very same physical and mental pleasure you had when it actually transpired.

In summary, while you wait your turn, take the opportunity to focus your energy inside, not outside. Your ability to change the outcome of the game once you have lost control of the table is zero, but your ability to change your self-confidence and your actions once you are back at the table is unlimited.

In boxing, the one-minute break between a round is an opportunity for the fighter to recharge and refocus for the next round. While the boxer sits there looking at his opponent across the ring, the trainer will tell him to take deep breaths while the corner man massages the boxer's neck to rid him of any tension. Despite all the chaos that surrounds a championship boxing match, you can be sure that, between rounds, the champion will always be relaxing and focusing on his God-given talents. His confidence will remain high, no matter how bad he might appear on the outside.

So the next time you have to leave the table, don't beat yourself up and start directing your energy outwards. Rather, take the time to become centered on your mission: to win, one way the another.

Deep and regulated breathing can also significantly refresh the mind and help you think clearly. It is these short recharge moments that can give you the competitive edge, especially in a long tournament match, or in a game where your opponent is slow. Such focused breathing can lead one to a meditative state where the mind becomes calm, and that is always good.

It doesn't matter how good a player you are; at some point in time you will give up control of the table. The negative player will see a return to the chair as a defeat. But the champion, just like a boxer, will see it as an opportunity to refocus and recharge before coming out swinging again with even more vigor and authority than before.

Spiritedness

Webster defines the word "spirit" as: "Energy, vivacity, ardor, enthusiasm, courage," etc., while the word "spirited" is defined as: "Animated; full of life and vigor, lively," etc.

The word "spirit" expresses the essence of Universal Power and that which is present in man as the core of his being—his inner strength and power. Spiritedness does not mean the quality of being ethereal, spiritual, or otherworldly. It simply denotes a state of being "animated," or "possessed of vigor". This vigor comes from the very core of one's being—the "I AM" region or plane of consciousness. The quality of spiritedness is manifested in different degrees among different men—and animals. It is an elementary, primitive idiom of life, and is never dependent upon culture, refinement or education. Its development is a consequence of one's ability to recognize one's power within. And the more you can develop spiritedness, the better chance you'll have at winning in all areas of your life, what to speak of billiards.

Within the animal kingdom we see how the quality of spiritedness plays into determining who will be the alpha male. For example, if you put two male baboons in the same cage, rather than launch into an attack on one another, they will open their mouths to expose all their teeth and then proceed to 'blow' at each other. But one of them will blow with a hint of fear that immediately marks him as the inferior male and the "fight" is over. It is the same with the big cats. Put a dozen lions together, and they also, usually without a single strike, soon discover which one of them possesses the valor of the leader. Thereafter he takes the choice of the females. He becomes leader of the pride. It is not always the baboon with the fiercest teeth, nor biggest lion that asserts his dominion by winning a physical fight—it is always something far subtler than the physical—the self-esteem of the animal or its spiritedness.

And so it is with men. It is not the dog in the fight, but the "***fight in the dog***" that endures. The spiritedness or "nerve," or "mettle," of a man is always the deciding factor.

There may be no feeling of antagonism between you and your opponent, but there will be an inward recognition on both sides that one of you is superior. This superiority does not depend upon physical strength, intellectual prowess, social status or skill set, but upon the expression and recognition of one's inner power or spiritedness.

We often hear of people "lacking spirit"; or having had "their spirit broken," etc. The term is used in the sense of "mettle". "A horse with a "bigger heart" will always run a gamer race and will often outdistance and out-cardio a horse having greater physical characteristics, but less "spirit" or "heart". Other horses become discouraged and allow themselves to be beaten by higher-spirited horses, even though they may be superior physical specimens. This spiritedness or valor of an individual is a vital quality of success, but it can only be developed and strengthened once you become firmly established in knowing your higher self. Never allow someone else to define who you are. Believe in yourself and know that you are much more than what the world sees externally.

Sportsmanship
(Be a champion of character first)

There is nothing more appreciated in any sport than a humble winner or a loser who praises the victor. It's refreshing to see this because it focuses our attention on the most important aspect of any game, and that is respect. Such respect is often demonstrated in martial arts, wherein the combatants, after having given their best to maim the other, will respectfully embrace each other after the fight is over.

Respect is something we all crave. It is an inherent need of the spirit because it reminds us of our own true value and uniqueness. We are all unique. There will never be another person like us, and that is something we can always be proud of and thankful for. Only when we truly understand our uniqueness and self-worth is it possible to see it in others. The first thing in learning to be a good sport is being kind to yourself. Charity begins at home.

To put it another way, respect in equals respect out. Or conversely, garbage in, equals garbage out. What you invest in yourself will reflect outwardly to others. If we constantly beat ourselves up or consume negativity in the form of bad associations or media pollution, we can be sure that this same negative energy and disrespect will flow from us to all those we encounter. Similarly, if we think positively, speak positively, and generally feel good about ourselves, this same positive energy will follow us in our interactions with others. This is the basic law of karma, or as the Bible says, "*...for whatever a man sows, that he will also reap.*"[16] What you project will come back to either benefit you or hurt you. We all intrinsically know this universal law to be true.

Billiards, like all sports, can and should be a setting in which we build personal character, which includes integrity, respect,

---

[16] *New Testament, Galatians 6:7, 8.*

responsibility, and fairness. The essential elements of sports ethics are honesty and integrity.

Winning is a consideration, but not the only one, nor the most important. Remember, we all originally got involved in billiards for enjoyment, first and foremost. We should never lose sight of that core motivation.

Rather than striving to be the champion of the world, first strive to be a champion of character – a champion of integrity, honesty, and respect. Accept both victory and defeat with pride and compassion; never be boastful or bitter. Congratulate your opponent in a sincere manner, following a victory or a defeat.

Here is my five-step program for building a champion attitude:

1. **Always respect your opponent.** Make the effort to genuinely congratulate or encourage an opponent, putting aside all ego, reservations, and insecurities.
2. **Never demand respect.** Earn it through a professional and quality-driven attitude. Respect should be welcomed but not stolen.
3. **Believe in yourself**. You are absolutely unique and special. Your skills and character are uniquely yours and yours alone. Appreciate them and grow as a person to realize your true potential.
4. **Never allow others to control your reality.** The power others have over you is the power you freely give to them. Never allow others to define *your* reality.
5. **Speak positively**. Avoid all negative talk. Only voice what you want to see happen in your life now. Your words are literally molding your future, so choose them wisely. If you must refer to negative experiences, speak of them always in the past. Remember that words carry energy, and what you put out will come back to you.

If you follow the above program, I can assure you that not only will your entire outlook on life change for the better, but your friends and family will change as well, as they begin to value your integrity and your positive influence on their lives.

As Benjamin Franklin once put it:

> The best thing to give to your enemy is forgiveness; to an opponent, tolerance; to a friend, your heart; to your child, a good example; to a father, deference; to your mother, conduct that will make her proud of you; to yourself, respect; to all men, charity.

Mr Franklin certainly was a wise man and with true wisdom comes humility. Only a humble heart has the full capacity to learn, and thus the cycle of wisdom gathering rolls on without end.

In the classic book of Jewish ethics, *Duties of the Heart*, Chovot HaLevavot explains, "Humility is the ability to see reality," while Albert Einstein once stated:

> My religion consists of a humble admiration of the illimitable superior spirit who reveals himself in the slight details we are able to perceive with our frail and feeble mind.

It is wrong to equate humility with weakness. A heart that is filled with humility is one that is aligned with the essence of spirit. As we tap into the Source of our power and identity, it is natural to be humbled and want to extend respect to others, for we are all connected to that same Source.

In the *Bhagavad Gita*, Krishna states that when one learns to see this energetic Source equally present everywhere and in all living beings, he "does not degrade himself by his mind," and thus, "he approaches the transcendental destination."[17]

Another way to respect your opponent while building a likeable personality is to take a genuine interest in what they have to say. You'll find that too many people, particular in the West, go through life so absorbed in their own affairs that they project an impression

---

[17] *Bhagavad Gita* 13.29

of being aloof or uncaring. This "coldness" can be interpreted as selfishness; no one likes to hang out with a cold and selfish person.

By taking a genuine interest in people, by setting aside your own self-interest and listening to their story, even for a moment, you'll create a powerful impression on everyone you come in contact with. People will appreciate the respect you are giving them and reciprocate the same with you. In *The Secret of Success*, Atkinson says, "It is the Law of Compensation working on the mental plane – you get what you give".

It would be wrong, however, to make yourself a "welcome mat" for people to "wipe their feet on". Discretion is needed in how much quality time you give to others. Just keep in mind that there is no greater compliment you can give to someone than to listen to them well. As the golden rule states: Do unto others what you would like them to do unto you. That is respect.

The Power of Individuality

Individuality is inherent in every living being and is the expression of our Self—the sense of "I". Each of us is an individual "I" differing from every other "I" in the universe. To the degree we develop and express the inherent power of our unique "I", that much we will be successful in life. Individual expression lies at the heart of our success in everything we do, including billiards.

But before you will be able to apply this idea successfully, you must first understand what the Individual—the "I" within you—really is. This statement may seem absurd at first, but it will pay to familiarize yourself fully with the concept, for with realization of the "I" comes true power.

If you stop for a moment to take stock of yourself, you will find that you are a more complex being than you had at first considered. In the first place there is the "I" or consciousness which is the real Self—the Individual, and then there is the "Me", or that which is attached to and belonging to the "I". To clarify this, allow the "I" to take stock of the "Me", and you will find that the latter consists of three layers or principles, the physical body; the vital energy; and the mind. In a world where one's style, ethnicity, or social status are measures of worth, it is common for people to consider their bodies as the "I". But a little introspection will show clearly that the physical body is merely a covering, or "vehicle", through which the "I" is expressing itself. We never say, "I the body", we always say "my body", "my arm", "my head", etc., clearly expressing the fact that we are something higher than the physical body.

On the other side of the coin, one may be vividly conscious of the "I" factor while totally oblivious of the presence of the physical body, as in the case of dreaming. It follows then that the physical body is dependent on the "I" to function, just like a puppet is dependent on a puppeteer. Once the "I" departs from the physical body the body dies. The "I" however always remains constant while our bodies continually undergo change, including the final change at death when the body returns to the earth. Your body is composed of countless cells which are dying and being replaced at every moment of your life. Your body of today is entirely different from your body of a year ago. If my body is always changing, then who are you really? We can only conclude that you are the "I" within.

The second principle of the "Me" or physical identity is vital energy, or what many call *qi* (chi), *prana*, or the electro-magnetic current of the body. This energy appears to be independent but it too is in a constant state of flux and simply an instrument of the "I" to animate the body, and therefore only a characteristic of the "Me". Finally, we have the mysterious mind. It is easy to assume the mind to be part of the "I"; however, think for a moment and you will see that the mind is not you, but rather something that you use. What is that *thing* that is aware of your mental states, emotions, feelings, ideas and dreams? It is the real Self—the "I" which is superior to the mind and therefore uses it like it does with the body. You say "I feel"; "I think"; "I believe"; "I know"; "I will"; etc. You, the real Self or "I", are always above the mind. It is not the mind that knows, but the "I" which uses the mind in order to know. This may seem a little confusing if you have never made a study of the subject before, but contemplate these points a little and the concept will take root.

My agenda is not to bore you with metaphysics, philosophy, or psychology—there are plenty of books that go into these matters at length. My objective is to teach you that with realization of the "I" or true Self, comes a sense of indomitable power that will manifest in everything you do and bring out the very best in you. Realization of the "I" will develop a sense of knowingness and power that will enable you to not only express your individuality but also give you the necessary detachment required to execute shots with confidence and to not be adversely affected when things don't go your way. Also, until you understand the "I" within, you will never realize your true uniqueness.

The "Me" side of you is your personality—the external appearance of yourself. Your personality consists of countless characteristics, habits, idiosyncrasies, thoughts, expressions, fears, and beliefs. In essence, a bunch of peculiar and sometimes inconsistent traits that you have foolishly been thinking all this time was the real "I". Now you know better. Our character and personality can change at any time, but the "I" within always remains the same.

Did you know that the word personality originated from the Latin word "*persona*", meaning "a mask used by actors in ancient times". This word was actually derived from two other words, "*sonare*," meaning, "to sound," and "*per*", meaning "through". The two words combined mean, "to sound through". The idea being that the voice of the actor sounded through the mask of the assumed personality or character. The Webster Dictionary describes "person," as, "A character or part, as in a play; an assumed character."

Personality therefore means *the role you play* on the great "stage of life". The real individual, You, or the "I" is concealed behind a mask of personality. The higher Self that says "I AM," when you assert your existence is the true source of power.

The word "individual" denotes something that cannot be divided any further or something that cannot be changed by outside forces. You are an individual—a higher Self—endowed with a mind and body to use, as *you* choose. Embrace your individuality and rise to the "stage of life" with your head held high.

But, alas, while the external identity is not as important as the higher Self within, it still plays a crucial role in the drama of life because, as a rule, the audience gives more attention to the personality and physical appearance than it does to the real person behind the mask. Therefore, in billiards it may serve you well to cultivate a personality that is attractive and uplifting to those you interact with. Because no matter how self-realized we may be, if we wear the mask of an unattractive personality, we will be operating at a great disadvantage and drive away people that we might benefit from or who would be happy to help us if they could see behind that mask. An attractive personality is not synonymous with an attractive appearance. Rather, it is a persona that people feel comfortable with. However, you'll find that it becomes easy to cultivate such an attractive personality once you tap into your higher Self.

In billiards, like any sport, when we harness the unlimited power of our higher self, we set ourselves apart from the common man and literally take the driver's seat of life!

Enthusiasm

We instinctively know what enthusiasm is, but have you ever wondered from what source the word originated? It is derived from the Greek term meaning "to be inspired; to be possessed by the gods", having been originally used to designate the mental state of an inspired person who appears to be under the influence or inspired by a superhuman or divine power. However, it is now more commonly used in the sense of: "lively manifestation of joy or visionary zeal".

This secondary and somewhat misleading meaning of "visionary zeal; imaginative fervor"; ignores the primary source of enthusiasm. Real and sustained enthusiasm results from a connection to a higher source—a kind of "plugging into the power socket" experience.

A person filled with enthusiasm is inspired by a power higher than themselves by tapping into a source of which he is not ordinarily conscious. The result is a magnetism that radiates an attractive force in all directions and influences everyone. Enthusiasm is contagious and when fully experienced by the individual they become a source of inductive power – a center of mental influence. This mysterious power does not come from an external source but rather the inner regions of the soul or consciousness. Enthusiasm therefore is really "soul power", and when genuine, it is recognized and felt by everyone coming within its field of influence.

Without a certain amount of enthusiasm no one ever has attained success. There is no influence in personal interaction that compares to enthusiasm. By definition, it comprises earnestness, concentration, and unbridled power, and there are few that cannot be influenced by its manifestation. Rather astonishingly, however, few people realize the significance of enthusiasm and thus go about life either lackadaisically or with the "enthusiasm" of a fool. This is no more evident than in the attitude of a struggling billiards player, who goes into each match with an "enthusiastic" belief in their *inability* to succeed. This perverted sense of self-worth only serves to compound their distorted reality of lack and failure, which is so foreign to the spirit.

Note it down: **Enthusiasm is the power source that drives our mental machinery**, and thus directly inhibits or empowers us to accomplish great things in life. William Walter Atkinson explains it this way:

> *"You cannot accomplish tasks properly yourself unless you manifest a degree of interest in them, and what is enthusiasm but interest plus inspiration – Inspired Interest, that's what enthusiasm is. By the power of enthusiasm the great things of life are brought to expression and accomplishment."*

Enthusiasm is not the sole possession of a few lucky ones. Everyone potentially has it, but only a few are able to express it. The majority are afraid to let themselves "feel" this energy of enthusiasm and then allow the "feeling" to express itself in powerful actions like the spark in an engine.

Most players do not understand how to harness the fire of enthusiasm. This is because they fail to stoke the coals of interest and desire that are the source of enthusiasm. Cultivating a genuine interest and love of billiards develops enthusiasm. Interest, confidence, and desire arouse enthusiasm, but it remains for you to either direct it toward your goal of becoming a great player or allowing it to dissipate without result.

Like hot air, enthusiasm may be used to float a large object like a balloon, or uselessly dissipated. The more interest you take in learning all aspects of billiards, the greater your confidence and desire will grow—and from these arise the force of enthusiasm. Always remember that interest is the "mother of enthusiasm". The fact that you are reading this book clearly shows that you have what it takes to harness the full power of enthusiasm.

Enthusiastic players are naturally optimistic, believing anything is possible. Their attitude creates an atmosphere of confident, cheerful expectation, which serves to aid all his endeavors. Indeed, enthusiastic players surround themself with a mental aura of success—and those who associate with them unconsciously absorb this same vibration. Enthusiasm is contagious, and those filled with it unconsciously communicates his interest, earnestness and expectations to others. However, as mentioned earlier, if the enthusiasm is one centered on negativity, it has the opposite effect, bringing all who associate with it down, for "misery likes company".

Naturally, enthusiasm plays an important role in personal magnetism as well. It is a warm, vital mental quality that quickens the heartbeat of everyone affected by it. A person that has charisma is naturally someone that also possesses a certain quality of enthusiasm.

The player who lacks enthusiasm is cheated of much of his force of personal influence. No matter how good your technique may be—no matter how strategic and methodical you may be—unless you possess the warm vital quality of enthusiasm, all your efforts are largely wasted, and results weakened. Think of all the salespeople who have approached you over the years and how some of them lacked a certain "charm", while others caused you to listen and take notice in spite of better judgment, simply because of their earnest interest and enthusiasm.

Ideas that Inspire

When you are feeling a lack of enthusiasm, doubt, timidity, or fear, it means that you have too many mental inhibitions crushing your inner confidence. Kick them out of your mind and you'll immediately feel light, cheerful and optimistic again.

Sometimes, the thoughts that aroused enthusiasm in you one day, may disgust you the next day. Similarly, the thoughts that inspire one person may discourage another. Yet, there are some ideas that inspire all when men of zeal possess them. For example, the inspiring battle-cry of a great leader can motivate a totally dispirited army. Indeed, their mere presence can rouse a soldier to heroic achievements. Simple words like, "Liberty" or "Freedom" can make men do the unthinkable. These words are but the signs of ideas, yet the sounding of these ideas into consciousness can instill unlimited foot-stomping pounds of energy on the trigger of action.

And so it is with you and I. Deep down in the innermost chambers of our soul lie unearthed storehouses of energy just waiting to be unleashed. And when they are properly applied, they can totally transform your destiny. However, to harness these hidden treasures you must persevere. In a marathon race, the one who endures is the one who wins, not the light-footed sprinter that races out to the front early on. In the same way, life is a kind of marathon. There may be many "good starters," but few "strong finishers." That is why the failures far outnumber the winners.

To merely comply with the "norm" is a sure path to an average result. The progressive person, on the other hand, plans the day before; he delights in attempting more than the average; he loves his work more than he loves his pay. Of course, this attitude necessitates choosing a career path that you love, and this context, playing a form of billiards that you truly enjoy.

Most of us start playing billiards with raw enthusiasm. We play for hours on end, but soon enough, we run dry of the will-power to persist and eventually succumb to the lure of other interests and fail.

It is therefore imperative that you keep the passion strong in your hearts by associating with people that truly love the game and are also models of inspiration.

The next time you go to play billiards, take the time to analyze each player's enthusiasm for the game, and then see how much of a positive influence that player exerts around the room and on their own game. Then remember the effect it produces upon yourself, when you feel it. To be a champion you must be enthusiastic.

Always Learning
(A wise person can extract gold from a dirty place)

There is something divine in the fact that, despite all our learning, we never reach the end of knowing. The goal of complete illumination always seems just around the corner—just beyond our grasp. As in everything, there always seems to be someone else smarter, stronger, faster, or more skilled. New champions are constantly displacing current champions and there seems no end to how accomplished humans will become in any particular sport. Of course, the same applies to the game of billiards, and so it's worth our while to keep improving our skills and to fully embrace this fact.

Despite all their years of training, experience, and knowledge of the game, every true champion will aim to keep learning something new. In the same way, we should always keep our ears and eyes open to any little "nugget of gold" we can collect on any given day. It is no coincidence that we were born with two ears and two eyes, but only one mouth! Sometimes we just need to know when to be quiet and receive new information. And sometimes it can appear in the most unlikely circumstances.

For example, while observing another player, we may get all hung up about their fundamentals, or lack thereof, and dismiss them as someone we cannot possibly learn from. However, this would be a huge mistake, since each one of us has something to offer. We are all unique individuals, and it follows that no two people have the same set of experiences or knowledge to draw from. A smart pool player therefore will always be on the lookout for something to learn from their opponent, even if it is just their shot choice or attitude around the table.

Efren Reyes, arguably the greatest pool player in the history of the game, is said to have learned a lot of his creative genius by watching beginner level players create shots that most people would never imagine. Because of their inexperience they would "think outside the box", and it was this irreverence and breaking with the norm that enabled Reyes to earn the nickname, "The Magician" and become one the most exciting players the world has ever seen.

Legendary actress Eartha Kitt once said:

> *I am learning all the time. The tombstone will be my diploma.*

Her legend is as much about her entertainment skills as how she conducted herself in her public and private life.

The English biologist, Thomas Huxley, wisely advised:

> *Sit down before fact as a little child, be prepared to give up every conceived notion, follow humbly wherever and whatever abysses nature leads, or you will learn nothing.*

It is this sort of open attitude that defines childhood and makes that experience so mesmerizing and profound. In reality, despite our physical age, we remain children in the eyes of God and nature. The Earth was born some four billion years ago, and yet humanity's recorded footprint[18] on this planet is but a mere few thousand years. Truly, there is so much about this planet that we have absolutely no idea about.

Therefore, if you want to get on the "fast track" to improving any area of your life, you have to "stand in the sun" and seek out and associate with successful people you admire. There is nothing more valuable than to have the personal guidance of a master of an art. Billiards is no different. You need to either find a qualified trainer and take lessons, or at the very least, start playing against players of a higher ranking. If you don't, and prefer to just play against the same group of people day in day out, your game will never reach championship status.

---

[18] *Recorded history dates back to only the 4th millennium BC, with the invention of writing.*

It is often said that you can judge a person by the company they keep. This simply means that a person will typically become what their friends are. If we keep good company, chances are we will become good. If we associate with people of questionable character, however, it is highly likely that we will eventually adopt their same bad habits. Essentially, if you want to know a person, find out who their friends are.

One way to understand this is the following example:

If you visit a perfume shop your clothes will acquire a pleasant smell and create a positive experience for you and the people you interact with thereafter. However, if you visit a fish market your clothes will reek with the smell of dead fish and most probably offend those you come into contact with. Similarly, associating with pious or impious people will automatically result in you taking on some of their "karmic dust". Such is the nature of energy exchange.

A famous Chinese proverb states:

> *A single conversation with a wise man is better than ten years of study.*

I encourage you to be always on the lookout for "nuggets of gold" in billiards and in life. Never stop learning, for in billiards, and life in general, without the quest to learn with a humble and open attitude, life would be a bore and a terrible waste of human life.

Visualization

Ask any successful person, whether an elite athlete, entrepreneur, entertainer, or even a political leader, and one thing will ring true with every one of them—they have visualized their success before it actually happened.

"I just knew it," they'll tell you. "Somehow I could see myself doing it. I would dream about it, smell it, feel it, and practically taste it." Philippe Petite, the *"Man on the wire"* who famously walked between the Twin Towers in 1974 revealed that he actually desired to do this as a teenager when he read about the plans to build the Twin Towers in New York. At that time, the Twin Towers were just architectural drawings, but Petite was already visualizing himself walking between them! The desire became an obsession, and after years of preparation, including numerous flights from Paris to New York, exhaustive research on the buildings, and help from friends, he did what seemed impossible to everyone else accept him.

In the early morning hours of August 7, 1974 Petite walked between the Towers, some 450 meters above ground. With a sense of pride, Petite even toyed with the awaiting police officers by going back and forth between the Towers eight times, sometimes even laying down on the wire to "talk with the seagulls", he said.

It is this sort of creative visualization and focused intention that carries one to the desired goal. In the motivational classics *Think and Grow Rich* by Napoleon Hill, and *The Magic of Thinking Big* by David Schwartz, a large proportion of the subject matter is dedicated to visualization and the art of "faking it until you make it".

How can we apply these same principles to our game of billiards? Well, let's not get ahead of ourselves and start dreaming about winning the world championship when we are still struggling to run one rack of nine ball. Although we may have lofty aspirations, it is best to take it one step at time. In other words, set achievable mini-milestones along the way to your "Mount Everest" moment of glory.

Here is a simple exercise I want you to try out to improve your run-out capability. Take a notepad, get a red pen and a blue pen, and draw up a table on each page. Next, randomly draw nine circles all over the table. Number them 1 to 9. Now you have a nine ball spread. The good news is you have "cue ball in hand". So draw one more circle as your cue ball. Now, begin visualizing how you would run this rack. Using the blue pen, draw a line from your cue ball to the 1 ball and then from the 1 ball to the desired pocket. Now with the red pen, draw the path of the cue ball, and make an X at the point you would like your cue ball to stop for the next shot. Next, do the same with the 2 ball all the way to the 9 ball, using the blue pen to mark the path of the cue ball before contact, and the red pen to mark the cue ball path afterwards. Keep in mind that this exercise assumes that your run out enables you to move your cue ball around without disturbing your layout.

The idea behind this exercise is that it forces you to actually see the run out in your mind. You have no choice but to see the cue ball moving around the table, because you will not actually play this layout until later. This sort of mental exercise will help sharpen your run-out skills at the table. The next time you play, instead of scratching your head and getting flustered, you'll know exactly what to do. It will breed confidence in your game by helping you to see solutions and recall them as needed later on.

I suggest you do this exercise when you are away from the table; for example, on the train to work or while waiting at the doctor's office. Quickly draw up a layout and try to run the table. You may find that your layout is too difficult and you lose position after a few "shots". Don't worry, it's at these times that you can pretend you're Efren Reyes and pull off some magical shot of the century. Hey, it's *your* visualization, and no one has a right to tell you how you should play! So expand your creative potential and surpass all apparent limitations. Being successful means going beyond the norm to excel in some endeavor, and this all begins with seeing your success inside your mind.

Once you are in a habit of doing this exercise, take it to your poolroom. But this time, instead of drawing up the layout, actually spread the balls around the table. Now, without playing a single shot, hold your cue and walk around the table and see yourself running the rack in your mind. Don't hit any ball until you have run out to the 9 ball and the crowd is applauding you in your mind's eye. Once you've taken a bow, chalk up and play like the champion you are within.

Training Drills

Once you familiarize yourself with the Three-Cut System, aiming will become a natural and rhythmical part of your pre-stroke routine. You won't have to think about it nearly as much as you do now. Your instincts will guide your body into the proper alignment as you get down to play your shot. It is important to understand that, in essence, all shots are straight once you have the correct alignment. Play your stroke true to the alignment you have set with your body, and focus on positioning the cue ball for your next shot. That is what the pros do.

Down the Line

Here is a great drill to fine-tune your stroke so that you consistently deliver the cue ball in a straight plane without unnecessary sidespin.

Place a striped ball on the center of the half-circle at the head of the table. Now practice hitting the ball up and down the center of the table so that it runs over the rack spot and returns directly back to your cue tip, all the while keeping the stripe centered. This will necessitate that you stay down after executing the shot. If you can do this consistently, and then with your eyes closed, your stroke is at a championship level, and you can confidently proceed to the pocketing drills (Figure 12).

FIGURE 12

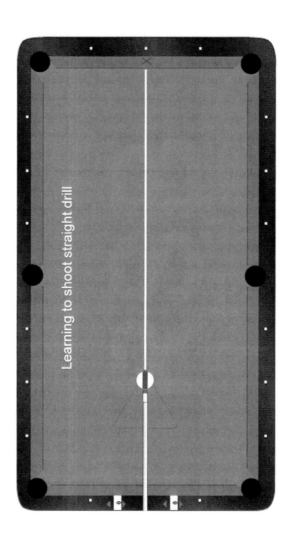

Learning to shoot straight drill

The Half Ball Reference

This drill is a classic one for teaching you the half ball cut. It is a drill that is often practiced by professionals during a warm up and is known as a "spot shot". If you keep at this, over time you will be able to pocket the ball repeatedly, even with your eyes closed. It is that predictable!

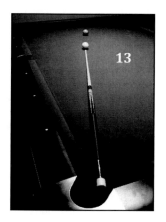

Here is how you set up a "spot shot" on a nine-foot pool table:

- Place one object ball on the foot spot[19].
- Place the cue ball in line with the object ball and just inside the corner pocket, as shown by the cue stick in (Figure 13, above). You can also place the cue ball two diamonds up from the end rail and one diamond in (less that the width of a cue ball) as shown in (Figure 14). This set up is a perfect **half ball** cut shot because the angle needed to send the object to the pocket is 30° degrees. By aiming for the left edge of the object ball you will send it into the far right pocket.

Other shots to practice

- For a **quarter ball** cut, place the cue ball two diamonds up and two diamonds in from the end rail (Figure14).
- For a **three-quarter-ball** cut, align your cue with the object ball and the point on the rail marking the fourth diamond. Anywhere along this line is a three-quarter-ball cut. You can also place the cue ball a distance of 3½ ball widths from the side pocket. A classic one-eighth cut involves placing an object ball (orange) one diamond down and one diamond

---

[19] *The spot on the table where the balls are racked.*

inside the top rail, and the cue ball three diamonds down and half a diamond in from the left rail. Again, you can align this cut by placing your cue over the object ball and the point on the rail marking the fourth diamond. Any point along that line is a one-eighth-ball cut (Figure 14).

After practicing each of these fundamental cut shots repeatedly, you will begin to see variations of these same shots in a real game, giving you a huge advantage over your opponent!

Cut shots that challenged you before will look rather easy, because you will be able to correlate them to one of the three fundamental cut shots. With regular practice, your eye will become trained to see these standard cut angles (14°, 30°, and 49°, or three-quarter, half, and quarter cut shots, respectively) and also recognize if the shot is slightly more or less than these reference points.

Once you practice the above standard cut angles, it is easy to create your own individual training drills.

The following drills will not only deepen your understanding of the Three-Cut System, but also help you to recognize standard paths of good cue ball control.

FIGURE 14

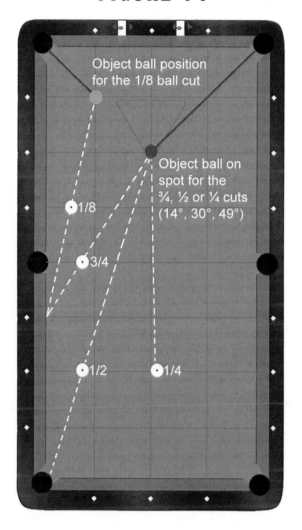

Three-Cut Training Drills

Drill 1

This setup is the exact opposite of the standard spot shot shown in (Figure 14). Place the object ball on the spot, then line up your cue ball so it forms a direct line with the middle pocket. A half ball contact on the right side will send it to the corner pocket, because this angle is 30°. Be aware of the *throw*[20] effect on this shot because of the long distance the object ball has to travel. (Figure 15).

Drill 2

Place the object ball in line with the first diamond from the corner pocket. Place the cue ball on the line from the object ball to the second diamond down from the opposite pocket. This will create a perfect half ball cut at 30° (Figure 16).

Drill 3

Set the shot up as for Drill 2, but this time focus on hitting the cue ball firmly in the center to create a "stun" effect. When the cue ball has no forward or backward spin at the time it contacts the object ball, it will slide off the object at 90°. The natural path of the cue ball is shown for such a stun shot. Practice this shot to get safely to the other end of the table without scratching. Your rail aim point is the area around the second last diamond at the other end of the table (Figure 17).

---

[20] *"Throw" refers to an object ball being moved off the line of its natural path after cue ball contact because of spin applied to the cue ball, or because of a split-second grabbing of the object ball when a cue ball collides with it at a sharp angle. In this example, the tendency of the object ball will be towards the rail, so you may have to aim slightly outside the right edge of the ball to make this. It should be noted, however, that throw is less influential on the lighter and smaller size billiards balls (2.125 cm) as used in snooker.*

Drill 4

This is a variation on Drill 3, only this time your goal is to make the cue ball hit the rail target area around the third diamond down table. You can do this by hitting your cue ball with topspin at a medium pace. This is a great drill for learning how to avoid middle pocket scratches (Figure 18).

Drill 5

This is a great shot to practice. By setting up the object ball in front of the center end rail spot, with the cue ball in line with the spot on the rail corresponding to 2½ diamonds, you will have a perfect quarter ball cut shot at an angle of 49° (Figure 19).

Drill 6

Play the same shot as in Drill 5, only this time hit your cue ball slightly below center to create a stun effect, so that it is sliding as it contacts the object ball. Try to make the cue ball go up the center of the table. This 90° rule applies any time you have a ball on or near the rail and when the cue ball is sliding into it (Figure 20).

Drill 7

This drill will help you to learn positional play-off balls on or near the rail. By playing the same shot again, striking your cue ball at the top to create some topspin, you will see the cue ball drift forward away from the 90° line. The trick is to do this while avoiding a scratch in the corner pocket. The same shot can be played with draw and will have the opposite effect, bringing the cue ball drifting back towards you (Figure 21).

Drill 8

Here we have another quarter ball cut shot. Place the object ball at the intersection of the first diamond on each rail. Now align the cue ball so that it sits at the same intersection across the table. Play this with a slow, smooth stroke. Be careful, because it is very easy to scratch in the side pocket. This drill will help you with speed control (Figure 22).

Drill 9

The same shot as in Drill 8 can be played more firmly to avoid a side pocket scratch. Hit the cue ball firmly in the center, or a little below center, to avoid the side pocket and go down table towards the rail target area of the second last diamond (Figure 23).

Drill 10

The same shot again, only this time you play the shot with stun and some authority so that the cue ball enters the position zone depicted in illustration (Figure 24). This shot requires a good sense of speed control to get the correct bounce of the 2nd cushion, but learning this shot will be invaluable in a game like 9 ball.

FIGURE 15

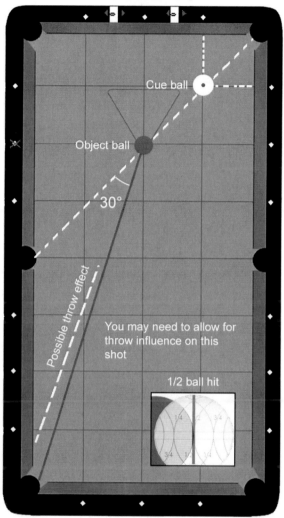

FIGURE 16

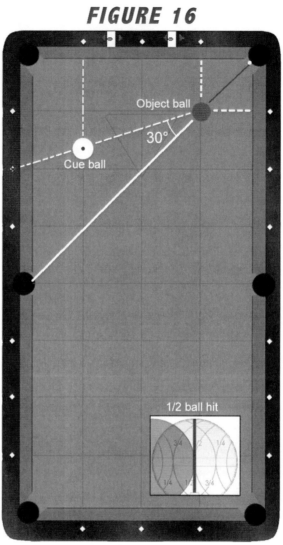

FIGURE 17

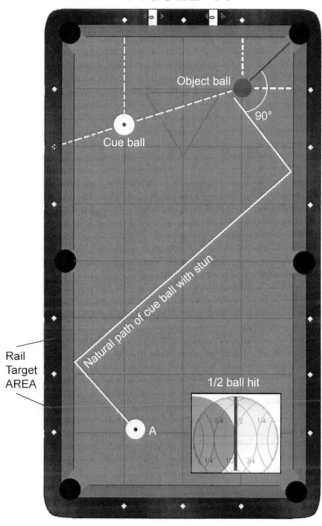

Object ball

Cue ball

90°

Natural path of cue ball with stun

Rail
Target
AREA

A

1/2 ball hit

3/4 1/2 1/4

1/4 1/2 3/4

95

FIGURE 18

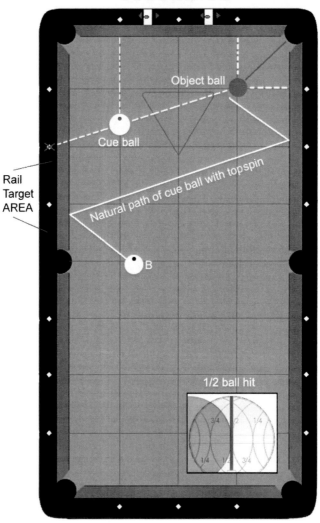

Object ball

Cue ball

Rail
Target
AREA

Natural path of cue ball with topspin

B

1/2 ball hit

3/4 1/2 1/4

1/4 1/2 3/4

FIGURE 19

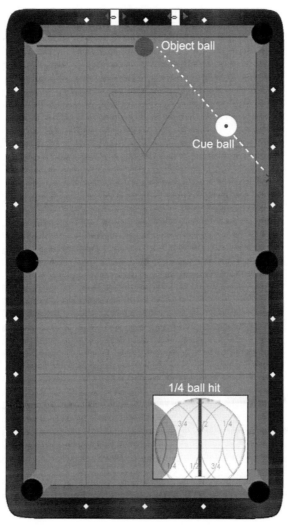

FIGURE 20

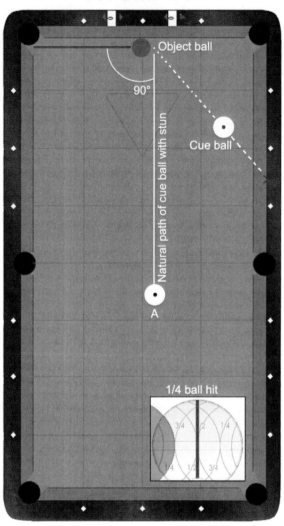

Object ball

90°

Cue ball

Natural path of cue ball with stun

A

1/4 ball hit

3/4   1/2   1/4

1/4   1/2   3/4

FIGURE 21

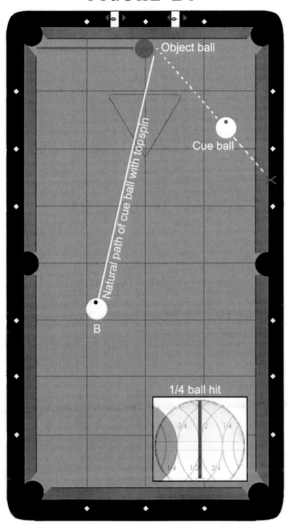

FIGURE 22

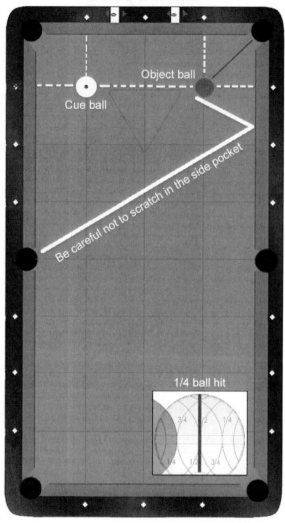

FIGURE 23

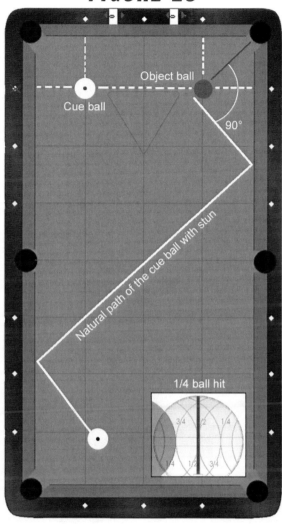

FIGURE 24

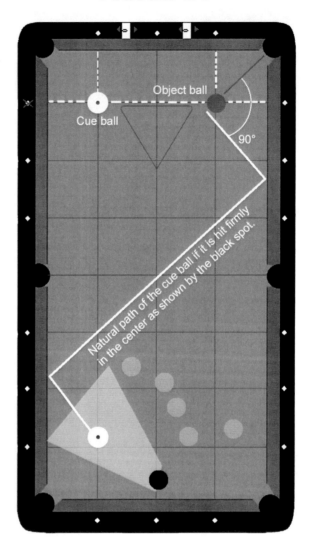

Object ball

Cue ball

90°

Natural path of the cue ball if it is hit firmly in the center as shown by the black spot.

Confidence Building Exercises

The following exercises, including some techniques used in neural-linguistic programming (NLP), will help you develop the self-confidence you need to augment your abilities. A player that moves with confidence around the table and in their dealings with others is always hard to defeat. Even if you have a greater set of skills, until you compliment those skills with a healthy dose of self-worth, you will play at a great disadvantage. *In billiards, confidence is King!*

Posture

As mentioned earlier, posture is important because if the body is not properly aligned your voice won't project with the power and a weak voice is fuel for the weak mind. When you speak to your opponent, you must do so with confidence. Not arrogance and disrespect, but confidence that you have the ability and will to win. A good posture will help to reinforce that feeling and make you that much more believable.

Be careful to always carry your head vertical and never to the left or right side, as to do so, indicates weakness. Strong men never tilt their heads. Their heads sit firmly on their shoulders. Every line on the body of a confident person will show strength. You'll find that when you make the effort to express confidence in your body language, it will not only earn you more respect but will cultivate a corresponding mental state within you. For just as thought precedes action, so too does action develop mental states. You need to think and act with self-respect and by law self-respect must come to you.

Exercise 1

Imagine there is a string that runs through the top of the head and down through the neck, then down through the spine. Then imagine that higher force pulls up slightly on the string, straightening the neck and the spine to the point where even if there were no muscles holding them in place the bones would stay sitting one on top of the other, and at the same time you feel your shoulders slide back into place. Now, imagine moving through the world this way, and more importantly when you walk around the pool table.

Exercise 2

In order for some people to keep their shoulders back they need to stretch out the chest and strengthen the back, especially the rhomboids (between the shoulder blades) and the rear deltoids (backs of the shoulders).

Posture Stretches

Number 1

This stretch should be felt just above the collarbone in that little triangular indention below the neck.

1. Stand with your lower back straight. Have your legs shoulder width apart, and your knees slightly bent.
2. Reach behind the back with your right arm and grab the left arm (which is down by the side) at or just above the elbow.
3. Rotate the left arm back in the socket gently, making sure you're turning the arm at the shoulder joint and not the elbow.
4. Turn your head to the right looking over the shoulder, and then tilt the chin down toward the shoulder.
5. Hold this position for 60 seconds.
6. Repeat on other side.

Alternate Step 3: If you can't reach your arm that way, just gently rotate the shoulder back in the socket without holding the arm. You'll know if you're doing the stretch right by where you feel it.

Number 2

1. Move your shoulders up toward your ear.
2. Roll them back, squeezing your shoulder blades together.
3. Let your shoulders drop, letting them stay back naturally.

Number 3

You'll feel this stretch in the chest, just below the collarbone, from the breastbone all the way to the shoulder.

1. Place the palm of your hand against a wall, with your arm straight and your hand about three inches above the shoulder.
2. Lean into the stretch, so your body is as perpendicular to the wall as possible while remaining comfortable.
3. Hold stretch for 60 seconds.
4. Repeat on other side.

You can also do neck and shoulder rolls to loosen up these areas and help them realign after the stretches.

Breathing

It's important to breathe in deeply in order to project your voice and have power and resonance. You won't be taking in more air, but you will be breathing into the lower portion of the lungs instead of into the upper portion of the chest.

Exercise 1

Put your hand on your upper chest. Breathe so that this part of the chest moves out when you breathe in. As you breathe out, let out a natural sound like "Haaaaaarah" with the breath. Now put your hand in the middle of your chest and breath into this area, and as you release your breath say "Haaaaaarah." Lastly put your hand on your stomach and as you breath in you should notice your stomach expand. Now say "Haaaaaarah" as you let the breathe out, but this time take notice how much stronger and resonate your voice is when you speak from here.

If this isn't easy for you, try holding your hands above your head while you do this. As a last resort you can lie on the floor and practice there so you know how it feels, before you practice standing up.

While you do this remember to keep your shoulders slid back and your back straight.

Emotion

When you speak it's important that you *hear* your feelings in the words that you say, otherwise you won't sound sincere. In the same way that you have excitement in your voice when you talk about thrilling experiences, or the wonder in your voice when you talk about unbelievable experiences, you need to enunciate words to complement their meaning. For example, if you were saying the word "short" you could make the word sound just slightly abrupt, or if you're saying the word amazing you could drag out the syllables a little and maybe even raise your voice slightly.

Exercise 1

Here is a list of emotions that you can practice saying with the feeling of the emotion in your voice when you say it. To help you out a little, you might want to imagine a time when you experienced this emotion, and see what you saw, feel what you felt, and hear what you heard. Also make sure when you imagine this event that you're looking through your own eyes and not watching yourself.

Love, sincere, amazing, excited, calm

Here's a list of words that would sound like what they mean

Huge, powerful, tiny, smoothest, rich, awesome

106

Exercise 2

You also need to practice using these words in sentences, especially since many of them might be in one sentence together.

Example:

> Have you ever made an *amazing* shot that seemed impossible?
>
> I was *playing* pool the other day and I saw the *smoothest* kick shot. It was *awesome*!
>
> I was so *excited* seeing the shot that I could hardly wait to try it out.

By focusing on these emotionally charged words when you talk, you will naturally develop a much more influential and believable speech pattern.

Exercise 3

Next time you watch a movie, try to ignore the words that they are being said and just take notice of what emotion the person is conveying while they are talking. You will find that as the states shift, the words will take on an entirely different meaning and feel, and in fact may not at all reflect the person's true feelings. By becoming aware of other people's tonalities, you can better understand what effect you're having on them regardless of what they may be saying!

Inflection

Your inflection is important, because according to how you use it you can seem powerful, or weak. There are three ways of speaking: commands, questions, and statements.

Statements will have a flat inflection at the end, *questions* go up at the end, and *commands* always go down. This is important to note because if you say something like, "Let's do this" as a question instead of a command, you give the other person a chance to say no. Also, a question isn't always a question. If you use the grammatical structure of a question but go down with the inflection at the end of the sentence, then you actually make it a command.

Inflection is also very important for being able to embed commands. You can embed a command using any note, but, for the sake of simplicity, here we're going to talk about embedding commands by dropping your tone slightly on the command. The difference doesn't have to be extreme, but should be slight so that it is only perceptible to a trained ear.

Embedded Commands

Embedded commands are used to say something to the unconscious while you might be saying something completely different to the conscious mind. You can do this by saying all of the words in the embedded commands in one particular note, at a particular volume, etc. The key is to have the note or volume that you embed the commands as distinct from the rest of what you say. For example, if you use the note *A Sharp* to embed the commands, you can't use that pitch elsewhere in your conversation. Personally I find it easiest to drop my pitch slightly on the embedded commands.

Example

You know I am going to win

> Hi, I have never met **YOU** before. I **KNOW** I have seen you around. **I AM** (your name). [Shake their hand while looking them directly in the eye] So are we **GOING TO** play? May the best man **WIN**.

I'm better than you

> **I'M** sure this table has **BETTER** cloth **THAN** the one I **U**sed yesterday.

Note: The command word YOU is created with the letter "U" in the word Used. The subconscious will pick up on the phonetic definition of first letter "u" (YOU) and ignore the last three letters "sed".

Have fun with this, but please don't abuse it. Remember, as I have talked about in the development of your Will, it is futile to use your Will on others. What is suggested here is as much about implanting confidence-building commands in your own mind as it is about planting "seeds of doubt" in the mind of your opponent.

Concluding Words

Billiards, like all sports, requires hard work to achieve lasting success. Many top billiards professionals these days not only workout regularly, but will also practice some form of meditation/visualization regime before a big match. Many of them will not admit to this, but they do it.

Gone are the days when you could get by with a few beers and bravado. If you want to compete at the highest level you have to get your body healthy; your mind sharp and friendly; both mind and body working in harmony; and most important you have to learn how to tap into your core inner powers.

I have given you the "ingredients" of what makes a great billiards player. Now it is up to you to execute them. Remember, pleasure is the purpose of life. If you are not experiencing happiness when playing billiards, it is most probably because your mind is distracted, or you are failing to tap into your core Self.

We go through life seeking pleasure of all kinds and for one reason or another we came to this peculiar game of billiards.

There is a reason for everything that happens, for this is a *feeling* Universe. Actions follow thought, and thought follows desire, and desire is fueled by Will, and the Will is the expression of our core Self, the "I".

I urge you to look beyond the externals of the game and seek to understand the deeper meaning of the geometry of life—the web of interdependence and interconnectedness of all things. The deeper we can go down the "rabbit hole", the more fascinating the drama becomes. What you want is to reach a stage of proficiency whereby your playing becomes like a dance. Your consciousness is fixated on the music within while your feet do all the work. Play billiards at that level and you cannot help but be successful, even in apparent "defeat".

May the lessons I have shared with you bring you happiness and success in billiards *and* in life!

The Billiard Aim Trainer ™

How many times have you said to yourself, "I wish there was a clear and simple way to know what the cut angle is?"

Enter the Billiard Aim Trainer (BAT™)[21], the world's first pool trainer that teaches the superior Three-Cut System of billiards.

By removing the parts of the cue ball that *never* come into contact with the object ball, and creating a cue ball that allows you to see right through it, we have created an aiming tool that is easy to use and quick to master. In no time, you will be recognizing cut angles at a glance and knowing exactly how to pocket a ball. No more guessing the imaginary "ghost ball". The BAT™ gives you immediate feedback, showing you what is actually taking place behind your cue ball. You get to see what the cue ball "sees!" Most amateur players have had no formal training in aiming fundamentals and often go on a "feeling" system. The BAT,™ however, can provide a solid foundation for aiming fundamentals.

The BAT™ sits on the pool table and uses a combination of references to show the player the exact cue ball path for targeting, the degree of the angle, the contact point, and exactly how much of the object ball needs to be cut. This patented invention requires no BAT™ batteries or technical skill to teach the key concepts of pocketing balls. Any person of any skill level can quickly become a better pool player within minutes of using the BAT.™

---

[21] *Also known as the Billiard Master in Asia. Available at DSBAT.com*

About The Author

Australian born Paul Rodney Turner (a.k.a. BATman) invented the *Billiard Aim Trainer*™ (BAT) in 2004 while contemplating a method to teach his billiard students how to understand and apply the three-cut aiming system he learned as a boy while practicing snooker.

Paul started playing pool in 1973 at the age of 10, on a seven-foot particleboard pool table in his family's garage. Fascinated by the art and geometry of billiards, Paul got his initial training from his father, Rodney Turner, a hustler in the pubs and clubs of Sydney who was affectionately known as the "Phantom" by his peers.

Paul eagerly studied the books of legendary snooker and billiard greats Joe Davis, Walter Lindrum, and Eddie Charlton. Soon afterwards, he became a fan of a new BBC series called *Pot Black*, featuring the new breed of snooker professionals like Steve Davis and Jimmy White. With a sense of optimism, Paul began practicing on 12-foot snooker tables for four hours a day, meticulously going through drill after drill to perfect his game in the hope of one day becoming a professional snooker player.

Then in 1983, as if called to a higher purpose, Paul put away his snooker cue and traveled East to study the ancient mystical teachings of India. It is that experience that Paul now draws on when explaining the more metaphysical aspects of billiards, like mind management, enthusiasm and gamesmanship.

In 1995, Paul founded Food for Life Global (www.FFL.org), the world's largest vegan food relief organization, with projects in over 50 countries. He still directs the charity from his home in Australia.

Paul did not pick up a cue again until 2002, when friends encouraged him to try out nine ball. Drawing from his past snooker experience and his extensive study of the art, Paul quickly established a reputation among his peers, and soon many of them began asking for personal training.

In 2006, Paul founded the Billiards Training Company to manufacture and sell his invention, the Billiard Aim Trainer™ http://www.billiardaimtrainer.com, which is endorsed by the Billiards Congress of America (BCA) and used by professional coaches and thousands of amateur players all over the world.

Paul continues his study of the art and science of billiards, and has been personally trained by world champions Allison Fisher and Gerda Hofstatter, as well as by top touring pro, Max Eberle, and Master BCA instructor, Jerry Briesath.

In 2010, Paul released *"The World's Best Aiming System"* to explain the three-cut system to his students and customers.

For personal training, send an email to paul@billiardstraining.com.

Bibliography

Bhagavad Gita As it Is, A.C. Bhaktivedanta Swami, (original edition)

Savor, Thich Nhat Hanh

Duties of the Heart, Chovot HaLevavot

Think and Grow Rich, Napoleon Hill

The Magic of Thinking Big, David Schwartz

Essential Skills, Kim McFarland and Tom Vizzini

The Secret of Success, William Walter Atkinson

The Secret, Rhonda Byrne

BilliardsTraining.com

Made in United States
North Haven, CT
16 September 2023

41635847R10065